A MODERN

INTERPRETATION

OF JUDAISM

A MODERN INTERPRETATION OF JUDAISM

———

Faith through Reason

CHARLES SCHWARTZ

BERTIE G. SCHWARTZ

SCHOCKEN BOOKS • NEW YORK

First published by SCHOCKEN BOOKS 1976

Copyright, 1946, by The Macmillan Company
Copyright assigned 1954 to Charles and Bertie G. Schwartz

Library of Congress Cataloging in Publication Data

Schwartz, Charles, 1892-1969.
  A modern interpretation of Judaism.

  Reprint of the ed. published by the National Women's League of the
United Synagogue of America, New York, under title: Faith through reason.
  1. Judaism. I. Schwartz, Bertie G., joint author. II. Title.
BM565.S37 1976   296   75-35447

Manufactured in the United States of America

To Our Children

Stuart, Louise and Ernest

FOREWORD

THERE is a belief generally prevailing that faith and reason are contradictory terms. It is thought that, like oil and water, they cannot be mixed, that each is inconsistent with the other, and that in terms of religion, faith excludes reason; that faith in a religious sense, is beyond and outside the realm of reason.

The authors do not agree with these views. On the contrary, it is their deep conviction that religious beliefs need not be taken on hearsay and that faith need not be arrived at blindly. It is their considered judgment that the test of reason may be applied to both, that religious beliefs may be adopted and that faith may be reached through the intellect.

There are, of course, certain phases of religion and faith that are not susceptible to complete explanation through the mind. But in these instances, we human beings have the right to insist that these conclusions as well, even if they cannot be made entirely subject to the test of reason, at least shall not violate our sense of reason and logic.

The religious beliefs and faith taught by Judaism can, in the writers' opinion, be arrived at largely through reasoning. This does not mean that the beliefs of Judaism alone can be supported by reason. Reason can also be applied to beliefs upon which Christianity is based. These two great religions, the religions that have made the most powerful impact upon our present civilization, include a number of principles which are similar. These principles are mentioned in Chapter XXI entitled Jews and Christians—Relationship.

Thus it is one of the aims of the authors that, although this book is confined to an exposition of Judaism as it is interpreted today, the reader, whatever his religion, will be helped in reaching complete conviction in his beliefs and faith through a reading of this book.

The other aims and purposes that are sought to be accomplished by this book are set forth in Chapter I entitled Viewpoint.

CONTENTS

xi

Contents

A MODERN

INTERPRETATION

OF JUDAISM

Chapter I

VIEWPOINT

RELIGION is divine, but organized religion is a human institution. Organized religion has been developed by man in his desire to satisfy his spiritual longings.

Like all human institutions, it is subject to variances because of changing physical and social conditions, changing viewpoints, education and personal experiences. All of these have a fundamental effect upon a person's outlook on life and his religious and ethical behavior.

As life goes on, there is a constant change of ideas—so it is with organized religion. Religion grows as the human mind grows and religion constantly re-adapts itself and is re-interpreted to meet the needs of the times.

Judaism is no exception to the rule. Some of its principles and theories have changed through the centuries. The views and principles as understood and expressed by the prophets, by the rabbis and by scholars, over the years, vary in some respects from those originally embraced and set forth in the five books of Moses. Judaism shows a continuous process of testing and sifting, which has been going on down to the present day.

Any attempt to set down in writing, in simple and definite form, the principles of Judaism, becomes involved because of these changing concepts over the years. Judaism, however, is and should be based fundamentally

1

upon those principles which have been set forth in the five books of Moses. These books are the first five books of the Scriptures, consisting of Genesis, Exodus, Leviticus, Numbers and Deuteronomy. They are known as the Torah, and are sometimes referred to as the Pentateuch, and they are the cornerstone and fountainhead of Judaism.

This does not mean that each and every statement contained in the Torah must be taken literally. These books must be studied and understood, having in mind the primitive conditions existing among the Jews when the Torah was received by Moses on Mount Sinai. It is proper to take the principles, as enunciated at that time, and interpret them in the light of the conditions of today.

This point may be illustrated by the Federal Constitution. The Constitution was adopted at a time when the conditions of our country were radically different from those of today. Yet, without in any way fundamentally deviating from the principles laid down by it, the Constitution has been interpreted by our Supreme Court in terms of the conditions as they existed when such interpretations were made.

In arriving at a proper interpretation and presentation of the principles of Judaism, later sources, such as the books of the Prophets and the other books of the Scriptures have been used. The thoughts and views of the scholars over the centuries down to the present have been considered; and there have been included in such studies, the teachings of the present-day synagogues, orthodox, conservative and reform.

The beliefs of Judaism are rooted in the Torah but are

not restricted by it. They are as free as any other phase of life—to be developed, to be improved and to be interpreted—as our civilization and man individually develop and improve. Just as human knowledge and understanding have grown, so organized religions have grown, and this applies to Judaism.

This book does not attempt a learned dissertation, in which each assertion is supported by reference to or citation from a sacred source; nor does it attempt to take each phase of the beliefs embraced in Judaism and point out the variations and changes in the understanding thereof through the ages or as differently interpreted from time to time by the prophets and scholars. It is rather a statement in a general way of the basic principles in the light of our present civilization and society. It is Modern Judaism—Judaism, what it means and what it stands for, today.

Of necessity, any outline of the principles of religion must be affected and influenced by personal views and beliefs. Moreover, no group of persons, of the same faith and even of the same division of faith, has entirely the same concept of its religion. Nor does this book attempt to enunciate the principles that would be fully approved of, either in whole or in part, by all rabbis.

The book is rather a statement of the principles as the authors understand and interpret them to be, and is an attempt to set them forth in simple, layman language, shorn largely of philosophical and metaphysical discussion. The authors are laymen, in no way connected with the rabbinate, who, after much study and thought, have had the impulse to put into writing these principles, so that persons interested in understanding Judaism, as it is interpreted today, can find such information available in brief and simple form.

Among those who may be so interested are included Christians as well as Jews. Christianity is the offspring of Judaism, and many of its principles and beliefs have been largely derived from Judaism. Thus, a study and knowledge of Judaism, of its principles and the reasoning underlying them, may be helpful to Christians in reaching a better understanding of their own religion and its ethical teachings.

There is another purpose which this book seeks to accomplish. There are many Jews whose views and thoughts of religion are vague and uncertain. They grope in the dark. They are disturbed and uneasy and in the hearts of some of them there is even fear, when their minds inevitably at times turn to religious thoughts. This book attempts to help to clarify these thoughts and to straighten out this thinking, and to open more widely and deeply the minds and hearts of those readers, to receive, accept and to practice the precepts of this great religion. With their minds and hearts so opened, the authors are confident that disturbance, uneasiness and fear will disappear and life for them will become fuller, brighter and sweeter.

There are also those who are unmindful of their religion and who profess Judaism mainly because of accident of birth or because of loyalty to their parents. This book may aid in inspiring them to make their religion a real and vital part of their lives, and thus enable them to derive the satisfaction and joy that a true understanding of religion will surely give to them. It is the hope of the authors that "Faith Through Reason" may provide the spark to start these persons on their way to a more profound study of their religion.

Without religion life is inadequate. We may not realize this inadequacy until we acquaint ourselves with religion. It is the same as in other phases of life. Those persons denied the good fortune of having children and the great joy experienced in rearing them, and the blessing of their love and affection, do not and cannot realize what they miss. In the same way, to appreciate the serenity of one's being, the inner peace, dignity, and zest of living that come to one who truly understands and practices his religion, one must experience such practice.

Finally, the reader is reminded that this is a book on religion—that it is not always simple or easy to project by the written word, religious concepts. Religious concepts are intangible, nonexistent in the physical sense, and incapable of definite measurement. To overcome to some extent these difficulties, technical and theological expressions have been avoided and illustrations have been chosen based upon our present modern daily experiences.

In order to secure a more complete understanding of the principles which are set forth, and to develop a better spirit of understanding, it is earnestly suggested that this book be read in a slow and deliberate manner, that the reader place himself in a contemplative frame of mind and reflect and ponder upon the thoughts presented in each chapter before proceeding to the next.

Chapter II

JUDAISM—IN GENERAL

JUDAISM is fundamentally a way of life. It is primarily concerned with life itself. It outlines the laws which should guide each individual during his lifetime, compliance with which will bring to him maximum happiness in life. Judaism speaks of the benefits that are to be derived during life. It is not interested in any advantages to be secured after death, as a reward for the manner in which we have conducted ourselves during life. Life is of prime importance.

There is nothing in the Torah that recognizes any heaven or hell. There is no provision for reward or punishment after death. Judaism does not cajole by promises of reward in the hereafter, nor does it threaten with eternal punishment. There is no promise of the retention of identity and personality after death. It is as if God had said, "Do not worry about the hereafter, follow my laws, obey them and comply with them, and then life will be good to you and the hereafter will take care of itself." The kingdom of God is not in heaven, but on earth.

Man is not born in sin but on the contrary, he is born in goodness and holiness. Sin does not cast any shadow upon man. Man is given freedom of will. His soul enables him to choose between good and evil. He can exercise his will to live righteously or in sin. If he sins, it is man's own choice, and he then brings upon himself unhappiness and affliction. If he lives righteously, then joy is the keynote of life. It is the joy that comes from doing what God asks us to do. If we comply with His laws, we shall find the world good and life worthwhile.

Judaism is opposed to austerity in life. It condemns the monastic idea of withdrawal and separation from human society and from worldly affairs in order to get into closer communion with God. Man is a social being and must not separate himself from his fellow man. Judaism frowns upon asceticism and abstinence from enjoyment. God's laws are not intended to mar life or to make it gloomy, but on the contrary, to enhance the value and the enjoyment of life. Man is encouraged to make life beautiful and to give it strength and vigor.

If man lives as God wants him to, he will have God's unfailing presence with him and he will experience an inexplicable inner security, and doubt and fear will disappear. The basis of man's relationship with God is that of love. It is akin to that of a father and his children. He loves us as if we were His children. We love Him as if He were our father.

The ethics are directed toward the individual's behavior with respect to all persons—not confined to Jews alone, but to all their fellow men. Justice, righteousness and charity must be practiced toward all peoples. Each person is commanded to love his neighbor as himself.

God is not the God of a particular family, nor is He a tribal God, nor even the God of one nation, but He is the God of all mankind, the God of the universe. We are all descendants from a common ancestor and every man is our brother and neighbor, whom we must love as ourselves.

Judaism preaches the brotherhood of man. The goodness of God is not for the Jews alone, but for all peoples. When Isaiah spoke of the coming of the Messiah and the reconstitution of the Jews as a nation in Palestine, he said that all the nations of the earth would come up to the mountain of the Lord, to the house of Jacob's God, so that He might instruct all peoples in His ways and to walk in His paths.

Judaism teaches justice, righteousness and peace, for all mankind—that all human beings are brothers, one in spirit and one in fellowship, that all are the children of the one God. Judaism teaches that the Jews have been selected as an instrumentality of God to bring about this happy state of affairs, that the Jews will make their contribution toward attaining this goal, not by proselyting nor by the sword, but by precept and by example, that by their conduct they will influence humanity to live righteously and in the spirit of God.

Judaism is a democratic religion—God is always available and accessible—it is as if God were the head of a large organization, the door of whose office was always open to all employees (the human race). There is no anteroom through which one must enter. There is no secretary who must grant the interview. There is no partner who must introduce you to the head of the office. Anyone desiring to enter need not be announced. Any member of the organization, having a complaint or problem or request to make, may freely enter and talk directly with Him.

Each human being is in direct contact with God through his soul. God can be reached simply and directly, without the intervention of any spirit or person. One has only to call upon God, he has merely to think of Him and communication is instant.

It is as if there were a direct line of telephonic connection between God and each individual and by thinking of Him, the individual has made connection with God, he has opened the wire for communication—with God on the other end of the line.

Judaism is a mature religion. It is a religion which appeals greatly to adults—to those whose minds have reached maturity. It is a logical religion whose true follower believes in it, not because of blind faith but largely because of its appeal to the reasoning power of his mature and logical mind.

There is nothing in Judaism that forbids man from reaching his faith in this manner. On the contrary, God has given him an intellect and a soul to enable him to arrive at faith with the help of his reasoning powers. Religious beliefs do not allow themselves to be commanded; they are and must be based upon conviction. There are, however, some beliefs upon which Judaism is based, that cannot be arrived at solely through reason. This is so because the intelligence and knowledge of each human being are limited to finite things, beyond which his mind cannot go. He can reason as to the correctness and logic of such beliefs up to a point—beyond that, he cannot comprehend. Beyond that point, faith to the extent that it is based on these beliefs, arises rather from man's inner urge and desire to believe. But beliefs arrived at, even in this manner, must not be inconsistent with or be opposed to reason. Accordingly, in Judaism, faith is based upon such beliefs as are arrived at through reason or such as are consistent with reason.

The religious impulse is instinctive in each of us. It is a very part of our being, of our soul. It is stored away somewhere in our remote consciousness. By becoming religious, by thinking of and contemplating God, we bring this instinctive religious feeling to the forefront and it assumes a definite, distinct and important place in our consciousness and personality.

We might say that our religious instincts become buried in dust when we fail or neglect to heed them, but that they always have within them the potentiality of becoming very much alive and active. When we begin to contemplate God regularly and in an orderly way, we throw off the dust and religion becomes a real and living part of ourselves.

Chapter III

THE NATURE OF GOD

JUDAISM is probably the first religion whose conception of God was that of a deity not clothed in terms of physical attributes.

Prior to Judaism, objects of worship were largely physical, like idols, or consisted of physical forms of nature, like the stars, the sun, the moon, or of natural phenomenon, like fire, rain, wind. God was often thought of as an enlarged human being, in terms of human physical form, stature and organs, including eyes, mouth and hands. Judaism gave to the world the concept of an incorporeal, a purely spiritual God.

That there is a God, we cannot doubt. As we look about the world, we see everywhere, order, intelligence and purpose. All the natural laws, like those relating to physics, to chemistry, to biology, to geology, are completely orderly, and given a certain state of facts, these laws will always operate in the same manner.

The phenomena of life in the human, animal and plant worlds—with birth, life's greatest miracle, and with growth, reproduction, decline and death—all follow definite rules and principles and all point forcibly to the fact that they are all part of some complete, intelligent scheme and plan and do not owe their existence to chance. The most minute part of matter, which can be seen only under the most powerful microscope, functions in accordance with known and well-defined laws.

All of the foregoing leads to the irresistible conclusion that there are order, intelligence and purpose throughout the universe. If we admit such order, intelligence and purpose, we must then admit that there is some supreme force or cause which exercises its influence to bring about these conditions.

Such a force cannot be haphazard, for if it were, it could not create in an orderly, intelligent or purposeful manner. Therefore, this force likewise represents order, intelligence and purpose. It is creative, directive and purposeful. This force must exist not only within the universe itself, but must exist outside of the universe, that is, outside of nature, or supernaturally, since reason tells us that it could not create something unless it existed before and outside of that which it has created. This force is supernatural because it is beyond our limited physical and intellectual faculties and comprehension and outside the sphere of created beings, and it is this supernatural force which we embrace in the word, God.

All we can say is "that He is" and not "what He is."

God is infinite and He cannot be described in finite (human) terms. We cannot liken Him to anything physical. Since we can only use our imagination within the limits of our mind, we cannot imagine God, who is beyond our finite mind.

On the other hand, we must not think of God as some impersonal, blind power or force. We human beings cannot worship something which is impersonal. Our hearts and souls hunger for something real, warm, pulsating and life-giving, having understanding, sympathy, kindness and love. Accordingly, our prayers are directed to the non-physical but existing, living and loving God.

Since the essence of God is unknown to man whose conceptions are, of necessity, colored by his own nature, we can describe God, in a finite way, only by stating those finite concepts which we consider Godly.

Many words and phrases have been used by the prophets, scholars and others in their attempt to give some mental picture of Him. These express the impressions produced upon us by the different acts of God's limitless being and nature, stated in human terms. These descriptions must all be taken in a figurative sense. They are the result of the desire of the human being to satisfy his normal longing to describe God, which he can do only in finite terms, the only terms he knows and understands. It must, however, always be borne in mind that these expressions really do not describe God but rather the impressions produced upon us by God, and they describe qualities which we consider Godly.

Judaism has no catechism. It was natural, however, for attempts to be made by scholars to organize and set down in writing the basic principles of the religion as understood by them.

One of the great scholars who undertook this task was

Moses Maimonides, who lived in the twelfth century of the present era. Six of his principles have reference to the existence and nature of God. The attributes that Maimonides ascribed to God, directly or inferentially, have been generally accepted as representing the views of Judaism in relation to the existence and nature of God.

These attributes so ascribed to God are grouped as follows:

The first embraces the thought that God is the Creator and Ruler of the universe. It is the recognition and acknowledgment that there is some force or power which is the cause of all beings. In the earlier part of this chapter, there has already been given the reasoning upon which this conclusion is based.

The second concept of God is that God is incorporeal. He is not a body. He is intangible. He has no physical form. He is not a force in the natural sense. He is unlike anything that can be pictured, visualized or comprehended. The principle of incorporeality is known in nature. Most of the forces that function within nature have no breadth, height or width, and cannot be seen. An illustration of this is gravitation. Another is electricity. We may see the results or the effects of such force, but the forces themselves are intangible. So it is with God. We can see His works but He Himself is unseeable.

The third attribute of God is that He is eternal. God always was, is and ever will be. Continuity of existence in perpetuity is likewise evident in nature. Science tells us that matter is indestructible. What we call destructibility is merely change. When we burn a piece of paper, the matter is not destroyed. The compounds of elements which go to make up paper have changed by the application of fire into other forms of matter, some gaseous and some solid. There has not been, however, any destruction of matter. It is this quality of continuity of existence in perpetuity, which we ascribe in the highest degree to God.

The fourth attribute is omnipotence. God is all powerful. He is the fount and source of all force, of all power. God's power is without limitation. Nature and the entire universe derive their power and force from Him and operate and act in accordance with His will and purpose. We arrive at this attribute of God, instinctively. It is evident by our spontaneous desire for prayer when we or one of our loved ones are in grave danger. We plead to God for help. Unless God is omnipotent, has the power to help if He so desires, prayer would have no meaning and the instinct to pray would have no purpose. Knowing that the entire universe is purposeful, we must believe that God has this attribute of omnipotence.

Fifth, God is omniscient. By that we mean that God is aware of the thoughts and actions of man. He is all-seeing, all-knowing. He is not limited by time. The past, present and future are revealed to Him. He is not limited by space. His presence and power are everywhere. He pervades and permeates the universe. In our very limited finite way, we also have to some extent this Godly attribute. In our mind's eye, we can recall the past, see the present and survey the future, and we can encompass the world. The panorama goes through our minds as if the events were occurring again. If we were to multiply this power of ours by infinity, we would arrive somewhere

along the road of God's power. It is this power that brings
us to the belief that God has a personal interest in each
human being. It is from this attribute of God that we derive our belief in an ethical code, that certain of our acts
are right and others are wrong. We derive our sense of
responsibility to a superior being based upon this attribute. If God were not aware of what we were doing, if
He were not interested in our acts, why should there be
any sense of responsibility to some superior being? Why
should we be concerned whether our actions are right
or wrong? The answers to these questions must be that
God is omniscient.

Lastly, there is the concept of the unity of God, that
God is one. This principle represents the belief in monotheism, the belief in one God. Judaism is the first religion
to conceive of a single universal God. This is the outstanding element of Judaism. Jews acknowledge and proclaim
this belief in all their prayers and in all solemn moments
of their lives, in the words: Hear O Israel, the Lord our
God, the Lord is One. Judaism is the purest form of monotheism. God is complete, perfect and self-sufficient. He
is One. He is not divisible nor is He made up of parts.
Judaism acknowledges God as the one and only God and
does not recognize as divine any power other than Him.
Judaism deems as inconsistent with this ideal, any split-up
of God's unity, by the recognition of any human being
as divine or of some intervening force or power between
God and man. If we humans are to believe, as we must,
that there is order, intelligence and purpose in the universe, we must believe that there is some single transcend-
ing power which brings these about.

As we survey the world and come to understand more fully the workings of nature, we appreciate how little man has learned about it. We have only to view the discoveries, inventions and developments in the fields of medicine, physics and chemistry, during the past one hundred years, to realize how much more progress there can and undoubtedly will be made in the generations to come. When we consider these enormous advances, accomplished in the short span of a century, it becomes apparent that life on this earth, in the sense of our knowledge, has just barely begun.

The foregoing applies equally as well to our knowledge of God and His ways. Man is merely on the threshold of learning and understanding the part God plays in human affairs. As generation follows generation, and as our spiritual, moral and intellectual capacities develop and broaden, so will our understanding grow, of this Unseen Power—permeating the universe within and without—this force we call God.

Chapter IV

FREEDOM OF WILL

THERE is no predestination. It is fundamental in Judaism that man is a free agent and may choose and pursue any course of action or conduct. Man has the absolute right of free inquiry, the use of his reason, the ability to investigate and to envision the possible consequences of his acts.

God gave freedom to man's will so that it could assert itself freely— Man has freedom of choice— He has freedom of self-determination— Man can take the initiative — He can reflect upon what he is about to do and can decide to do or not to do the contemplated act— Man can do what is in his power to do, by his nature, by his choice and his will.

God has given us the ability of controlling our emotions and instincts to afford us the opportunity of using self-control, thus enabling us to work out our own salvation for good or for evil.

If this were not so, all precepts would be useless, since man could never choose to do what was commanded nor abstain from what was forbidden— If every act were preordained, there could be no duty, there could be no sense of responsibility, since every act would then be done regardless of our desire and we could not prevent ourselves from doing such act, whether it be right or wrong.

If we assume that one of God's purposes in creating the world was to bring happiness to human beings, we must then adopt the theory that man is perfectly free in his actions, so that his good acts or evil deeds are of his own considered choice. If man's actions were pre-determined, then he could not select good from evil, as all would have been fixed in advance by the Divinity.

God does not want human beings to be mere automatons or puppets whose every act is controlled through strings pulled by Him. God does not believe that happiness can be achieved by human beings created with these characteristics. God intends that each human being should develop his own personality. For these reasons He has given to us freedom of will—freedom to choose between right and wrong, good and evil.

Broad basic laws have been laid down by God for the guidance of the universe, with complete freedom of action and choice on the part of the individual human being to conduct his life as he sees fit. If, however, in the course of such freedom of action, any human being violates these laws, he brings upon himself and upon other human beings, distress, misery and even destruction.

It can be said that God has created these laws and has given to the human being freedom of action within their boundaries, and from that point on, the human being is left on his own. We can imagine these laws to constitute the four walls of a room. The human being is placed within the room and has complete freedom of action within the limitations of the room. We can imagine these walls as being charged with electricity. As long as the individual keeps within these laws—stays within the four walls of the room—and does not break these laws—does not attempt to break through the walls—he will secure the maximum of happiness from life. If he attempts to break through, he meets with disaster.

In the case of gravitation, a person jumping from a window will descend toward earth regardless of any personal objections to the laws of gravitation. He may rail against gravitation and shout to the world that he disregards and will disregard gravitation. Nevertheless, when he jumps through that window, he will descend at a rate increasing thirty-two feet per second—per second, and nothing can check that fall unless some other physical law is availed of, which will counteract the force of gravitation.

In just the same manner as these physical laws are inexorable and inevitable, so the moral laws are immutable, and any violations of them will bring grief to the human being.

Wrong and wrong-doing, therefore, cannot be ascribed to God, but solely to man's own voluntary act. All happiness as well as all evil and affliction are brought about by himself and upon himself.

There are causes and events which help to shape and which in some respects affect the human being's freedom of decision. His surroundings influence his present and future behavior. Man is to some extent an imitative animal. The conduct of his parents, his brothers and sisters, family home life, and other factors have a fundamental effect upon his will. Heredity, environment, society, poverty and wealth, all have their varying effects.

Nevertheless, in the same manner that the human being has the ability and freedom to decide to comply or not to comply with the laws of the land in which he lives, he has the free will to comply or not to comply with the laws of God. In other words, a man is as much a free agent religiously and ethically as he is socially and politically. In all these instances, if he conforms, he is taking the road which leads to happiness and to life; if he fails or refuses to conform, he is on the road to unhappiness and destruction.

It is stated in the Torah that God has set before each human being the choice between life and death, the blessing and the curse. In the book of Deuteronomy, Moses, speaking to the Israelites, says: I call heaven and earth to witness against you this day, that I have set before thee life and death, the blessing and the curse; therefore choose life, that thou mayest live, thou and thy seed; to love the Lord thy God, to hearken to His voice, and to cleave unto Him; for that is thy life, and the length of thy days.

Chapter V

THE SOUL

THE Torah makes no direct reference to the nature of the soul or its origin or its relationship to human beings.

The term, life, embraces that form of animation which is evidenced by the process or cycle of life—birth, growth, decline and death. Life is part of and permeates humans, animals and plants. In this respect, they are all the same. Life gives rise to the basic elements associated with it —reason, emotion, instinct and the ability to propagate. One or more or all of these elements are found in humans, animals and plants.

The contact of life with the outside world and the development of its potentialities are gained through the physical senses—sight, hearing, touch, taste and smell— one or more or all of which likewise are part of human, animal and plant life.

Human beings are, however, more than a mere bundle of reason, emotions and instincts. There is something beyond this package. The human being appears to possess certain abilities completely absent from animal and plant life. These are—firstly, a realization of the infinite or divine, that is, God, and—secondly, an innate sense of right and wrong, of good and evil, with conscience as its guide.

As to the ability of realizing the infinite, it is indisputable that no matter what a man's belief, whether it is affirmative, as in the case of the person believing in a deity, or negative, as in the case of the agnostic or atheist, there is, nevertheless, in every individual a realization of the unlimited vastness of the universe above and beyond him and of the order which appears to govern it.

There is likewise in each individual this innate, this instinctive ability to distinguish between right and wrong, good and evil. When we commit a serious wrong, we require no education, no worldly experience, to tell us that we are doing wrong. We know that the act is wrong. We know that to slay a person in cold blood is wrong. On the other hand, we know that to volunteer aid to one who has been injured, without thought of compensation or reward, is to do right.

It is essentially these two additions to life which differentiate the life of the human being from that of animal and plant life. These two qualities or abilities—the ability to contemplate the infinite and the ability to distinguish between right and wrong, good and evil—are derived from the soul.

The ability to contemplate the infinite gives rise to what may be generally described as our religious instincts, the instinctive religious feelings of the human being. Our awareness of God, our love of Him, our adoration of Him, the urge to pray to Him, to have contact with Him and to seek divine help or guidance, and our thoughts relating to the meaning and purpose of life and to immortality, our personal religious experiences—all come through the soul.

The innate ability of the human being to distinguish between right and wrong, good and evil, is the basis of our moral instincts. This quality of the soul represents our natural sense of knowing what is right and what is wrong. From this comes our conscience, which is the sense or feeling of the moral goodness or badness of our intentions or conduct, and our sense of an obligation to do that which is right.

The word, moral, when used in this manner, is in contrast to the word, ethical. Morality has to do with the instinctive, natural-born feeling of what is right and what is wrong. Ethical conduct has to do with our view of what is right and wrong, based not necessarily upon an instinctive natural-born feeling, but upon intellectual judgment. Moral—has reference to that force which comes to us through our soul, without regard to any intellectual knowledge derived from education or worldly experience. Ethical—embraces the principles that we adopt and comply with, which have been derived through our intellect.

The word, moral, as we have used it, has no reference to the colloquial use of the word with reference to sex. It is used in its broad sense, relating to conduct generally—of conforming to just conduct, of conforming to the dictates of the moral sense—that is, of complying with the instinctive quality which we derive from the soul, of enabling us to judge between good and evil, right and wrong.

Thus, the soul gives us both the religious and the moral content of our personality. We need no education, we require no extraneous knowledge, to possess these two instincts, derived from our soul. They are part and parcel of our personality upon and from birth. They are with us as long as the soul is within our physical being, from birth to death.

We can, by observation, by study and by self-control, develop these qualities implanted within our soul, so that they will be deepened and broadened. Judaism teaches that these two attributes of our being are among the most precious of our possessions and must be developed by each of us to the maximum of our capacity.

Knowing that we humans are imperfect and need help in perfecting these qualities, God has helped us along the way, and has given us guidance. By means of revelation through the prophets, and by inspiration through the intellects of many other individuals, God has caused these religious and moral qualities to be formulated for the benefit of mankind into detailed rules and regulations for human behavior. These are the religious and ethical laws taught by Judaism.

To the extent that we have a soul, the human being has a part of God within himself, and is Godly.

The soul, being part of God, is intangible. It is something that cannot be measured with a yardstick or weighed on a scale. It has no material substance. It is not comprised of chemicals. Yet, it pervades and permeates the body and mind in the same manner as God pervades and permeates the universe. God is the universal soul, and one part of such universal soul pervades and permeates each living person.

Another parallel can be established between God and the soul by the thought that as the world is filled with God, so the human being is filled with the soul.

There have been times in the writings of Judaism when

a distinction has been drawn between "spirit," and "soul," but such distinction has never been made quite clear and these terms are generally used interchangeably.

The soul may be said to be a fragment of the Divinity, and if that is so, it is pre-existent in the sense that it pre-exists the commencement of life in any human being. Upon birth it enters our being and when death occurs—the termination of the animation that we call life—the soul leaves the body. Being part of the Divinity, it returns to its source and is again embraced within God, the universal soul.

Since the soul is a part of God, it would seem that it retains no entity after death, but continues as part of God without any separateness or distinct division from God.

What is left behind, is physical matter, composed of chemical elements which have become inert, which have lost all capacity of functioning, as when life was present.

We may visualize this concept by considering God as an enormous ball of copper. The copper is malleable and fine strands of wire can be drawn out from the solid mass. These strands are never separated from the ball; they are not attached to, nor do they ever become detached from, but always remain as part of the ball. Each strand extends from the ball to and into a human being. The strand can be deemed analagous to the human soul. It is and always remains a part of the ball, and though never separated from it, nevertheless, so long as it remains a strand, it is a distinct entity. Upon birth, the strand is drawn from the ball and connects with the human being, and upon death, it is drawn back into the ball and is completely reabsorbed within it.

There is thus this independence of the soul from the body—during life it is our direct connection with God, and upon death it is reabsorbed into God.

It has been said that we and God have business together. This business is carried on through the soul.

We can conceive of the soul as a composite radio receiving and transmitting instrument, through which we communicate with God and through which we receive our communications from God. We tune in with God when we pray to Him and we thus become the sender and recipient of messages to and from God.

When we give ourselves up to the contemplation of God, our soul takes us into a region beyond our present physical world, into an unseen world. We transcend, we go beyond the limitation of finite thought, and we draw therefrom power, strength and wisdom. The operation of our soul in this manner is as real as the effect of heat and pressure on chemicals, causing them to change into other combinations. If we have been nervous, tense or worried, we can, in a few minutes, cause ourselves to become calm. This is not a form of self-hypnosis. Our soul actually goes to work on our finite personality, changing our human conduct and behavior. It is a deliberate and conscious change from our daily thinking to a communication with the infinite, through our soul.

It has been said that we can experience union with

something larger than ourselves, a sense of oneness with
the power beyond, and that, in that union, we shall find
our greatest contentment and peace. That union we make
and can experience only through our soul.

Chapter VI

GOD'S INTEREST—PERSONAL

THERE are times in every man's life when he is conscious of and feels a certain personal, indefinable relationship between himself and a superior being.

Judaism stresses the thought that God is a personal God. God is not disinterested, but is actually and directly concerned with and interested in each individual. Divine providence extends to every man individually and this is often expressed in one form or another in the Torah. We are God's children— He is our father. He will listen to us and help us. He is with them that revere Him and obey His laws. This is the phase of God's personality that justifies prayer and explains the relief and comfort that come from prayer and from one's personal appeal to God.

The child, saying his prayers before going to sleep, appeals to God as if God and he were friends; God being the all-powerful, all-understanding friend who will listen to his requests and comply with them.

It is the personal God to whom we appeal and on whom we rely, in times of great stress. When we have suffered the loss of a dear one, or when we are in danger of death, or when we are faced with grave responsibility, we turn to and appeal to God for comfort, help or guidance. This impulse, this tendency to turn to a personal God asserts itself naturally and instinctively. We do not feel strong enough or sufficiently self-reliant to face it alone.

It is to God that we address our petitions with hope and even confidence in the efficacy of our prayers.

If a man is wounded on the battlefield, he prays to God that he may recover and get back safely to his home and family. God may give him the urge or ability to develop that additional amount of strength which he otherwise might not have developed, to enable him to survive his wounds.

This does not mean that God will stop or suspend the operation of the forces of nature. It does not mean that a person falling from an upper story may have his descent suspended in mid-air because of his appeal to God. It does mean that God can help, if He so wishes, without necessarily violating the natural laws. He can impart by inspiration ideas to a person, cornered by a lion, which may enable him to get out of his predicament. He may give to the wounded man the impulse to call upon additional strength, to overcome the inclination to give in and succumb to his wounds.

God is nigh unto all them that call upon Him, to all that call upon him in truth.

There are those who quite naturally will question these statements. They will point out that life does not appear to work that way, that God does not appear to be close to and interested in the individual human being. They will give illustrations of cases where persons who have lived thoroughly good and holy lives have nevertheless met with great misfortunes. They will also give instances of men who have violated the laws of both God and man, and yet have apparently attained success and happiness in life.

It must always be borne in mind that, although there is this personal relationship between the human being and God, there is also a broader impersonal relationship. The laws that have been laid down by God apply to human beings generally. Thus, an innocent human being may be harmed by reason of the violation of these laws by other human beings.

When I commit a wrong, some innocent person may suffer because of my wrong. We are all brothers of one great family and the wrongdoing of one of us becomes the wrong of all of us. Each man is a trustee for the rest of mankind. His failure to comply with the laws of God may cause suffering to untold numbers of persons. Accordingly, until we reach that point in life where our society is perfect, individuals cannot necessarily expect to receive, religiously, as it were, their just deserts.

It has been argued that this feeling of a personal God, having a personal interest in the individual, is merely a matter of human conceit, that God is too far removed to take notice of human beings, that the individual is of little importance in the scheme of the entire universe. Moreover, it is asked: How can God, or why should God, be directly and personally interested in each individual and give him aid? It is asserted that with more than a billion human beings now living on this planet, with the billions that have lived and died, and that will be hereafter born, and with untold life, possibly throughout the universe, it is fantastic to believe that God could or would remember and be actually concerned with and interested in each individual of these billions.

This thought is not as far-fetched as it would appear. Consider this illustration: The population of this country is approximately 140,000,000, of whom 30,000,000 are required to pay federal income taxes. With such an enormous population and the tremendous number of taxpayers, it would seem to be impossible for the Government to detect any single individual violating the law, by failing to file his tax return and to pay income tax. Yet, few who attempt to violate the tax law are successful. The Government's organization is such that any individual who attempts to evade his tax obligations rarely succeeds in doing so. The law eventually catches up with him.

If this is true with a population of 140,000,000 persons, it is reasonable to believe the Government could be as effective with two, three or five times the size of the present population.

If, with our imperfect human system of Government, a record of each individual can be kept and so completely checked in connection with tax obligations that practically no one escapes them, why should it seem improbable that God, the sum total of perfection, can embrace all human beings, past, present and future, and be aware of the thoughts and actions of each one of them? If a man-made institution can maintain this personal interest in each individual, why should it seem improbable that God can do the same?

The interest of God in each human being has been further illustrated by a library. A person entering a library thinks of it as a whole. He does not know and he does not create in his mind an image of each book separately. However, the librarian, who has spent many years in caring for this library, has a completely different reaction when he enters the room. Each book is separately known to him, each book has been given individual care and attention and each book has a meaning to him which it cannot have to the casual visitor. We, individuals, are the books and God is the librarian.

Our soul is precious to God; He has made man master of the world; each person is a part of God—hence His personal interest. God is like a father. No matter how many children a father may have, each individual child is dear to him and his personal interest is concerned with, and he is solicitous of, the welfare of each one. God loves each of his children as if each were the only one.

As it is stated in the psalms, He has made each one of us but little lower than the angels and He has crowned each of us with glory and honor.

Chapter VII

REVELATION—PROPHECY
AND INSPIRATION

REVELATION is a fundamental belief in Judaism and Judaism is largely based upon it. Revelation was first made by God to Abraham and then to the other patriarchs, Isaac and Jacob. Thereafter, the Torah was given by God to the people of Israel by revelation through Moses at Mount Sinai. After Moses, there followed in procession the prophets whose declarations are contained in the Scriptures and are considered revelations made by God.

As revelation has been given through the Scriptures, it is appropriate at this point to briefly discuss these sacred writings.

The Scriptures, sometimes referred to as the Old Testament, consist of three general divisions. We have often referred to the first division, the Torah (the Pentateuch), consisting of the five books of Moses. The second general division, known as the Prophets, is subdivided into two groups. The first group includes the Earlier Prophets, six books in number, Joshua, Judges, Samuel, books one and two, and Kings, books one and two. The second group embraces the Later Prophets, fifteen books in number, three known as Isaiah, Jeremiah and Ezekiel and the remaining twelve known as the Minor Prophets, Hosea, Joel, Amos, Obadiah, Jonah, Micah, Nahum, Habakkuk, Zephaniah,

Haggai, Zechariah, Malachi. The third general division, known as the Hagiographa, comprises thirteen books, Psalms, Proverbs, Job, Song of Songs, Ruth, Lamentations, Ecclesiastes, Esther, Daniel, Ezra, Nehemiah and Chronicles, books one and two.

None of these divisions is devoted exclusively to one subject. They have interspersed history, ceremonial observances, proverbs, songs, prayers, visions, dreams, warnings, advice, the laws and their restatement in different forms of expressions. The Torah, however, is largely devoted to the laws and ceremonial observances—the Prophets, to visions, dreams, warnings, advice and restatements of the laws—and the Hagiographa, to history, biography, proverbs, songs and prayers.

The Scriptures in their present form, embracing the books above described, and their sequence of arrangement are believed to have been fixed during the period beginning in the fifth century before the present era, when the Jews returned to Palestine from the Babylonian captivity and ending in the second century before the present era. The Torah is believed to have been so fixed by the fifth century, the Prophets by the fourth century and the Hagiographa by the second century.

There are other books extant not considered sacred writings and excluded from the Scriptures, known as the Apocrypha, comprising fourteen books.

As has been stated in the earlier part of this book, the very core of Judaism is the Torah, and Jews must believe that the laws contained in the Torah have been revealed to them by God if they are to believe in Judaism.

The belief in revelation is built upon a sound and reasonable base. Although God has given man through his soul the innate sense of right and wrong, of good and evil, and the freedom of will which enables him to choose between them—nevertheless, right and good are all-embracing terms and detailed laws and standards must be formulated, to be complied with by man, if he is to live the good life. We human beings, however, are not perfect. We have not sufficient resources to do a fairly complete job and we need help. Since God desires that we choose goodness, it is logical to assume that He will lend us a helping hand, that He stands ready to assist us in accomplishing an effective result.

It is therefore reasonable to suppose that God has deemed it desirable on occasion to reveal His will through the medium of human beings. Communication between God and man, wherein God has selected some individual as the instrument upon whom He exerts His power and through whom He manifests His will concerning human beings, and enunciates such will to humanity generally, constitutes revelation.

It has always been and it will always be a mystery as to the manner in which the soul comes in contact with God, or how God comes in contact with the human being that He has chosen as His means of revelation—but that He does is a fundamental belief of Judaism.

In considering the prophetic and inspired portions of the Scriptures as revelations made by God for the benefit of man, it is not necessary that every word, phrase and sentence be taken as having been given to the human race

by God in that exact language. It must be remembered
that God has used human beings as His messengers in
conveying His instructions and laws. In Judaism it is of
the essence that all human beings are completely mortal.
No individual is supernatural or divine. Therefore, being mortal, they are subject to all human weaknesses and
frailties. The prophet, who has written down the message
which he believes he has received from God, couches it
in language, limited by his own command of language
and by his education, and he expresses it in terms of nature and science as he knows them.

Moreover, some of the prophets did not themselves
write down the messages received by them. The messages
were orally conveyed to one or more of their followers
who wrote them down, or the messages were transmitted
from generation to generation by word of mouth and finally set down in writing. In the process of transmission,
there may have been additions and eliminations and the
draftsmen who finally transferred the messages to the written word may, consciously or unconsciously, have added
to or subtracted from what they had heard.

None of the foregoing detracts from the prophetic
or inspired character of the works. After all, it is neither
the physical words, phrases nor sentences, nor the literary
character in which the work is set, nor even the wealth of
detail, which concerns us primarily. It is rather the basic
thoughts, the instructions and the laws that God has conveyed which are of primary concern.

The words—prophecy and inspiration—have often
been used interchangeably. An explanation of their difference in meaning and thought may be helpful.

The Hebrew equivalent of a prophet can be translated as meaning a mouthpiece. In other words, God has selected some individual as His mouthpiece to announce to the world God's instructions and laws. A prophet receives this communication from God either directly as the Scriptures tell us Moses did, or through a vision or dream as the Scriptures tell us was the case with other prophets. The person who has been selected is aware of the fact that he has been so selected by God, either because of the direct communication or because he has talked with God in the dream or vision, and has been instructed to make public announcement of the message he has received.

Inspiration means literally a breathing in. The person who has been inspired by God has had breathed into him the wish of God. The person so inspired is not aware of the fact that he has been selected. He has received no specific instructions to make announcement to the world. Thus, we speak of persons who make great contributions to mankind, whether in religion or in the arts or sciences, as having been inspired by God. Such individual has no knowledge that he has been chosen as the vehicle through whom God makes transmission to mankind. It is the work of that person and not his knowledge of selection, which helps to lead us to the conclusion that he has been inspired.

When this distinction is borne in mind, the apparent differences in viewpoints as to revelation held by the orthodox, conservative and reform divisions of Judaism disappear. The orthodox group, and to some extent, the conservative branch, believe that Moses conversed with God and that the Torah is God's message as given to Moses.

They hold a similar belief with respect to the transmissions from God through dreams and visions as announced by other prophets. The reform synagogue leans to the belief that the manner of the receipt of the messages of the prophets need not be taken literally, but it acknowledges their inspired character.

When it is considered, therefore, that prophecy and inspiration are merely different means by which the same result is accomplished—that God's communications have been received by the human race—the basic difference between them disappears and it becomes clear that all Judaism considers, as part of its basic tenets, that the laws announced by the prophets have their derivation in God and have been given by God to man for man's compliance with them.

We must remember that there is a little of God in each of us. The soul in each individual represents his portion of God within him. That is why the human being is so holy and why the wanton destruction of human life is one of the greatest sins against God. God undoubtedly had a purpose in giving to each of us a little of Himself. We can imagine one such reason to be that it is the means by which He communicates directly with us and it may very well be that this has been His means of communication with the human race.

We can imagine that God communicates with the human race not alone for the purpose of expressing the laws by which He wants us to be governed, but for other purposes as well. Persons endowed with rare talent may be deemed to have been selected by the Almighty as His in-strumentality, through inspiration, to give to the human race the uplift, the comfort, the solace and the happiness that many such gifted persons have brought to humanity.

The great composer, whose music gives solace and joy to the human race has a spark of the divinity within him which has been brightened by inspiration, by the touch of God. The great musician who interprets this music so that it can be heard and enjoyed by the human race may also be deemed to have had that spark illumined within him by God.

The great statesman, whose vision, understanding and courage have contributed to make this world a better place to live in, the scientist who has harnessed nature for the benefit of mankind and the physician who has solved the mystery of dread diseases which have scourged society, all have been helped along in their work, if not in fact started on the way, by the inspiration of God.

Blessed are they who, touched by the finger of God and given the spark of genius, have the realization that they are trustees and agents for God in the transmission of that genius for the good of the human race. If they corrupt or destroy their power of transmission by living in a manner violative of the laws of God, they sin doubly —against man and against God. If they make their con-tribution to the maximum of their capacity, they have carried out the will of God and have added their bit, to the accumulations of the centuries, for the betterment of mankind, and for the fulfillment of God's wish of bring-ing about a better world, in which all people will live in the spirit of God.

Chapter VIII

THE LAW—IN GENERAL

PEOPLE are innately good. However, it is a basic truth that there is a little bad in the best of us and a little good in the worst of us. It is the function of organized religion through a religious and ethical code, to reduce the little bad to a minimum and to increase the little good to a maximum. If we had the ability to think things through thoroughly, or the patience, the persistency or the time to do so, there would probably be no need of such a code. But since many of us do not have that ability and most of us lack the patience, the persistency and the time, we must be furnished with a ready-made code.

It is this that the Jews believe God has done for them and for all the members of the human family. He has given them a code to help them, to give them a lift. He has provided them with a code which is to be a guide for their behavior, one sufficiently complete to cover the relationship between God and themselves, between man and man, and for their own individual selves.

Although this ready-made code has been given to them, it must not be taken by them as something to be obeyed and complied with slavishly, whether they like it or not—without inquiry, without question. They have the right and are in duty bound to study it and satisfy themselves that it is based on soundness and reason; that it is something for their good and for the good of all mankind. Moreover, each individual should reflect upon it and develop a more complete understanding of its full meaning and its significance. In this manner, there will be compliance with both the letter and the spirit of the laws, thus enabling each person to derive the full benefits that are intended, through obedience to these laws.

God gave these laws to the human race, not to restrict the individual in his legitimate pursuits in life nor to create for him hardships or unhappiness. On the contrary, these laws were given in order that each human being might live a full and rich life and derive the maximum of happiness that life can give to him.

As has been stated in the earlier part of this book, Judaism is fundamentally a way of life. The laws are the sign posts, the directions for finding the right way.

We must remember that it is not enough for man to live physically. He cannot live by bread alone. He must have the love and affection that come with family ties and with friends and he must have the belief and hope that come with worship of and with love of God. Man's physical being may be fed with food but his soul must also be fed.

We must also remember that all humanity is a partnership engaged in a great enterprise, each individual being a partner—obligated to carry out his duties, no matter how insignificant or important, and each one becoming entitled to his fair share in the benefits of the partnership. If any one member of the partnership fails or defaults in the performance of his obligations, the whole partnership is adversely affected.

Accordingly, it behooves each Jew to live up to his religious and ethical code to the maximum extent of his ability for his own benefit and no less for the benefit of humanity.

This brings us to the laws themselves. These laws are embodied in the Torah, the five books of Moses. They consist of six hundred and thirteen commandments of which two hundred and forty-eight are positive and three hundred and sixty-five negative. They were given to mankind through revelation and they form the foundation of Judaism. These laws contained in the Torah are referred to as the Written Law.

There is also the Oral Law. The Oral Law includes detailed rules, regulations and decisions, based upon and supplementing the Written Law, handed down orally from generation to generation and finally committed to writing, arranged according to subject matter. Such writings are known as the Talmud. The Talmud, in turn, is divided into two parts, the Mishnah and the Gemara. The first part, the Mishnah, contains the rules, regulations and the decisions up to the time when the Mishnah was formally reduced to writing. The second part, the Gemara, embraces the interpretations and commentaries, that is, explanations of the contents of the Mishnah.

The relationship of the Written Law to the Oral Law (the Torah to the Talmud) is in some respects analogous to that which exists in our country between what may be described as statute law and case law. Statute law embraces the statutes or laws enacted by our federal congress and by our state legislatures, and the case law represents the decisions made by our courts in construing these statutes and extending and applying them to the situations arising in life.

The Talmud was put into writing over a period of three centuries, between the second and fifth centuries of the present era. Those portions of the Talmud which have reference to the laws are known as the Halakah, the directions for finding the right way—the rules of right conduct in life. The remaining portions of the Talmud cover history, prayer, tales, fables, philosophical and religious discussions and commentaries and these portions are referred to as the Haggadah. There are two Talmuds, the Babylonian and the Jerusalem. The Babylonian is by far the more important of the two.

Also included in the Oral Law are the Midrashim, which consist of interpretations and explanations of the meaning of the Torah and other parts of the Scriptures, in the form of commentaries, sermons and other similar expositions.

The words, Laws, Judgments, Statutes, Precepts, Commandments, Rules and Regulations are variously used and although having perhaps different shades of meaning, are all deemed interchangeable terms for the purpose of this book.

Foremost among the laws are the Ten Commandments. Just as the Torah is the very heart and soul of Judaism, so are the Ten Commandments the core and the fountainhead of its religious and ethical code. In a broad sense the Ten Commandments may be deemed to embody and embrace in their significance and application all the laws

contained in the Torah and in the other books of the
Scriptures and in the Talmud, and many scholars and
rabbis have adopted this viewpoint.

The laws can be grouped into three divisions, the first
covering the relationship between God and man, the second, between man and man, and the third, having reference to man's individual self. They have been so arranged
in the chapters following.

Under each such grouping there have been mentioned
those of the six hundred and thirteen commandments
contained in the Torah which are considered pertinent.
There have also been included, in each grouping, those
additional laws deemed to be corollary to or derived from
the Ten Commandments and generally included by the
sages among the fundamental laws which should govern
the lives of all Jews and all people who strive to live a life
of righteousness.

A number of the six hundred and thirteen laws have
been directly used. They have not been designated by
quotation marks, as most of them have been rephrased
either completely or in part, or phrases or sentences have
been omitted, in order to make clearer their meaning
and to avoid repetition. Some have been given, not so
much because of the specific matters therein mentioned,
but rather on account of their broader implications.

There has been omitted reference to many of the laws
which bear no relationship to present day life. Among
those so omitted, are those relating to sacrifices, the ceremonial laws, the laws of the priesthood, the laws having
special reference to the life of a nomadic, pastoral and agricultural people, and also such other laws which, because

of the changes in civilization, no longer apply to our contemporary world.

In some instances there have also been given excerpts from the rules and regulations contained in the code of conduct known as the Schulchan Aruch. This code, representing a compilation of the decisions, rules and regulations contained in the Talmud, is more fully explained in the chapters THE LAW—MAN TO MAN.

The purpose of the laws is to promote the spiritual, ethical and physical welfare of the Jews, and the rest of mankind—spiritually, by inculcating correct ideas of God, of man's duties toward Him and of His relationship to our world, so that man shall become holy, as He is holy—ethically, by providing the rules which are to govern the relationship of man to man and his own personal self, so that each individual will become righteous, as He is righteous—and physically, by enjoining upon each person, the observance of the principles of morality, the regulation and control of his physical appetites, the practice of temperate living and abstinence from excess in any form.

Judaism is not based on belief alone. It is also based on action. It is not sufficient to sincerely and devotedly believe in charity. Each Jew must actively and wholeheartedly practice charity if he is to comply with those of the laws which enjoin the doing of charity.

The special stress that is laid by Judaism upon doing and performing, can be better understood when considered in the light of the mission imposed upon the Jews.

In a subsequent chapter, there will be explained God's intentions in entrusting the Jews with a mission—the mission to help spread the knowledge of the oneness of God and of God's laws to the peoples of the earth, and to influence them, by precept and example, to accept the laws. Therefore, if the Jews are to perform their mission, they must not only believe in the laws but they must fully comply with them. Jews must not confine themselves to belief alone—they must do, they must act.

Chapter IX

THE LAW—MAN TO GOD

THE first three commandments and part of the fourth commandment express man's duties to God.

The First Commandment—I am the Lord thy God who brought thee out of the land of Egypt, out of the house of bondage.

The Second Commandment—Thou shalt have no other gods before Me. Thou shalt not make unto thee a graven image, nor any manner of likeness, of anything that is in heaven above, or that is in the earth beneath, or that is in the water under the earth; thou shalt not bow down unto them, nor serve them; for I the Lord thy God am a jealous God, visiting the iniquity of the fathers upon the children unto the third and fourth generation of them that hate me; and showing mercy unto the thousandth generation of them that love Me and keep My commandments.

The Third Commandment—Thou shalt not take the name of the Lord thy God in vain; for the Lord will not hold him guiltless that taketh His name in vain.

The Fourth Commandment—Remember the Sabbath Day, to keep it holy. Six days shalt thou labor, and do all thy work; but the seventh day is the Sabbath unto the Lord thy God; in it thou shalt not do any manner of work, thou, nor thy son, nor thy daughter, nor thy man-servant, nor thy maid-servant, nor thy cattle, nor thy stranger that is within thy gates; for in six days the Lord made heaven and earth, the sea, and all that is in them, and rested on the seventh day: wherefore the Lord blessed the Sabbath Day, and hallowed it.

These commandments impose the duty of acknowledging and recognizing that there is one God and none other; that nothing above the earth nor on earth nor in the sea shall be acknowledged or recognized as being a god. The second commandment applies not only to idols whatever their form, but as well to anything living or mortal. The commandment specifically mentions anything on the earth. There is nothing on earth to which the knee may be bent or which may be worshipped in any fashion. There can be no recognition of divinity, be it in any inanimate or animate form, other than that of the one God.

The name of the Almighty must not be mentioned in vain. His name may be mentioned but only in a spirit of holiness when we pray to Him or when we consecrate ourselves to Him or when we take an oath in His name, or when we do a good act or deed in His name or for His sake or when we commit ourselves into His hands in times of trial or distress or upon the approach of death.

It is blasphemous to use His name in jest or in profanity or in testifying falsely after taking an oath in His name or to revile Him. The first law of holiness is to revere God and to revere His name.

The Jews are reminded by God that it was He who brought them out of the land of Egypt, out of the house of bondage. They must ever be grateful to God and express to Him their gratitude for this and His many other kindnesses shown to them. These commandments are intended to impose upon Jews the duty of always keeping before them the fact that God has given them the ability to pursue their lives as His children, freely and in accordance with their conscience.

The Jews are also reminded that because they have been given this freedom by God, they must exercise it in accordance with God's will as expressed by His laws; that it must be exercised in furtherance of righteousness so that the Jews and all mankind shall have contentment, justice and peace.

Jews must also trust in God and have faith in Him. As He saved them from the Egyptians and as His protecting arm was outstretched over them during their sojourn in the desert, so will He everlastingly guide them, protect and help them. As Moses submitted himself to God's will, so must they submit themselves. So that when their limited finite mind and body fail them, they can safely lean on Him, place their trust and faith in Him and submit themselves completely to His will.

We must love the Lord our God with all our heart, with all our soul and with all our might. This love does not mean an abstract love, mere utterances from the lips in private prayer or public worship. We must develop within ourselves a real, true and deep affection and love for our God. Even this, however, is not enough. We must show our love for our God by acting righteously.

A number of the commandments end with the statement, "Thou shalt fear thy God." We are thus com-

52 A MODERN INTERPRETATION OF JUDAISM

manded to fear the Lord our God. The word "fear" is not
used in its ordinary sense, that of being afraid. The
thought underlying the use of this word is that of reverence, of awe, and some translators of the Scriptures
have used the word "revere" in place of "fear." When we
meet an exalted personage, or one of extraordinary talents, or one who has performed some unusual deed of
heroism, we respect and admire him. If a single individual combined all of these qualities and achievements,
then we would be in awe of him. We realize God's all-
powerfulness and the other transcendent qualities we
ascribe to Him. We feel completely overwhelmed in our
relationship with Him. It is unthinkable that we should
violate His commandments. This is the meaning intended by the use of the word "fear."

It is interesting to note that in our relationship toward
our parents, we are instructed in the book of Leviticus to
fear them. Ye shall fear every man his mother and
father. The word "fear" when used in this connection
conveys a meaning in some respects similar to that intended when applied to God. It means that we must respect and revere our parents, that we must give heed to
their advice, instructions and directions.

Accordingly, to fear God is to revere Him, to be in awe
of Him, to obey Him and to comply with His laws.

Jews are reminded that they must keep holy the seventh day, the Sabbath day, not only because they, their
sons, daughters, man-servants, maid-servants, their cattle
and the stranger within their gates, may have surcease

from labor one day each week and thus be enabled to regain their full physical strength, but also because the Lord made the universe in six days and rested on the seventh and blessed and hallowed the seventh day.

By this commandment God has made the Sabbath day a reminder that He is the creator of the universe and the creator of all human beings, and on the seventh day Jews must recall their debt of gratitude to God for creating the universe and for creating each of them.

It is for these reasons that the Sabbath day is considered the holiest of the days of the year with the exception only of the Day of Atonement.

In pointing out by the first two commandments that there is one God and none other, and that He is the God who brought the Jews out of Egypt, God has required the Jews to set aside, in addition to the Sabbath, special days of the year on which they are to recall these commandments and to dedicate and consecrate themselves anew to Him and to His commandments. These special days are embraced in three holidays. They revolve around the exodus from Egypt, the giving of the law to the people and the sojourn in the desert.

The first is Passover (Pesach) commemorating the Jews' departure from Egypt. The celebration extends over a period of eight days (seven days in the reform synagogue). Synagogue services are attended on the first and second days (the first day in the reform synagogue), and on the last two days (the last day in the reform synagogue). The Seder is conducted either on the first two evenings or on only the first evening, and there is complete abstention from eating leavened bread during the entire period. The Seder is a meal at which, in symbolical manner, the Jews are reminded of their enslavement by the Egyptians, of the hardships imposed upon them, of the punishments visited upon their oppressors to induce them to permit the Israelites to leave and of the exodus under the leadership of Moses.

The second of these holidays is The Feast of Weeks (Shabuoth). During the third month after their departure from Egypt, the Jews arrived at the foot of Mount Sinai where God then revealed to Moses and to the Jews the Ten Commandments and the other laws and regulations. This event is celebrated on two days by participation in the services of the synagogue. The services revolve about this momentous event in the history of mankind. In the reform and in some of the conservative synagogues there has developed the custom of confirmation. Boys and girls, of the age of about fourteen, participate in the services in a dramatic and musical program. The Decalogue (the Ten Commandments) and its meaning and significance are stressed in the expectation that a deep impression will be made upon the children and that they will remember to live up to this great bill of rights throughout their lives.

The third holiday is The Feast of the Tabernacles (Succoth). This holiday, extending over a period of seven days, commemorates the sojourn and wandering of the Jews in the desert for forty years until a new generation of free men was born, destined to enter the land of Canaan to build a great nation. Jews celebrate this holiday by building arbors (Succoth), symbolic of the dwellings used by the Israelites in the desert. They attend services in the synagogue and in these arbors, on the first two days (one day in the reform synagogue), voicing their thanks to God for preserving their people.

During the period when the Jews were an agricultural people, these holidays were also considered symbolic of the different stages of the harvesting, and the prayers on these holidays include those of thankfulness for God's bountifulness to them.

In a broader sense, these holidays have a deeper meaning to the Jews and to all mankind. Passover is symbolic of freedom—it is the message that God wants all humanity to be free and that freedom is the sacred right of all human beings. The Feast of Weeks is symbolic of justice and righteousness—God has given to mankind laws which, if obeyed and performed, will insure to each human being just and righteous treatment, the inalienable right of all peoples. The Feast of the Tabernacles symbolizes God's eternal presence on earth and His interest in all peoples—each person is assured of the ever presence of God and of God's guidance and personal interest in his welfare if he will only seek God with his heart and soul.

In addition to the three holidays, the Torah has fixed certain days as the solemn days. They are New-Year (Rosh ha-Shanah) observed for two days (one day in the reform synagogue) and the Day of Atonement (Yom Kippur). Attendance at the synagogue is required. The period commencing with the first day of New-Year and ending with the Day of Atonement is known as the Ten Penitential Days. During this period each Jew takes spiritual stock and inventory of himself. He searches his mind and his heart to discover wherein he has sinned—wherein he has failed in his duties to his God, to his fellow man and to himself. He prays for God's forgiveness and he couples his prayers with sincere regret for his acts of omission and commission and he deeply resolves thenceforth to live in accordance with God's will. When, on the Day of Atonement, he makes confession and prays for forgiveness, he confesses and asks for forgiveness both for himself and for all Israel.

The most stirring part of the synagogue service on New-Year is the blowing of the horn (Shofar). Many meanings have been ascribed to this rite. The one generally accepted is that it is the public announcement by the Jews to God that they have opened their hearts and minds to Him to make confession of wrongdoing, and of their resolve thereafter to conduct their lives as He has willed.

The Day of Atonement is a day of deep humility, spiritual cleansing and high resolve. It is the holiest day of the year. Jews fast on this day so that the physical hold of the body on personality will be loosened, thus making easier communion between their soul and God. The keynote of the day is that repentance is not enough but that there must be a real and deep internal change, a sincere resolve and determination to turn over a new leaf and thereafter live in accordance with God's laws.

There are minor holidays and fast days commemorating historical occurrences in the history of the Jewish people subsequent to the period embraced by the Torah and therefore omitted from it. The better known ones are the Festival of Lights (Hanukkah), commemorating the victory of the Jews over the Syrians, under the leadership of the Maccabees, in the second century before the present era; the Feast of Purim, recalling the rescue by Queen Esther of the Persian Jews from the destruction plotted by Haman, the Grand Vizier, believed to have occurred in the fifth century before the present era; and the Fast of Ab (Tisha B'ab), a day of sorrow, the anniversary date of the destruction of Jerusalem and the Temple by the Romans, in the first century of the present era. Although these holidays and fast days are historical rather than religious, their observance has great value. Their observance focuses the attention of the Jews on their history as a people, thus helping to maintain a warm and deep Jewish consciousness.

There are also certain rites and symbols which are prescribed by the Torah. The rite of circumcision is performed to carry out the covenant made with God by Abraham on behalf of all future generations of Jews. The symbols which are to be constant reminders to them of their relationship with God are: Phylacteries (Tefillin), placed on the head and bound around the left arm during the morning prayers; the Fringes (Tsitsit), attached to a vest, worn under the clothes throughout the waking hours; the Scarf (Talith), worn over the garments when praying; and the Doorpost Symbol (Mezzuzah), attached to the entrance of the home. The Phylacteries, the Fringes and the Scarf are worn only by men.

The Phylacteries are a reminder of God, of the individual's relationship with Him and of the duty to comply with His laws, when he starts the day; the Fringes act as such reminder to the individual during his waking hours; the Scarf, when he prays; and the Doorpost Symbol is such reminder upon entering or leaving his home.

All Jews observe the rite of circumcision. Most of the orthodox and conservative Jews attach the Doorpost Symbol and use the Scarf while praying, especially in the synagogue. Many of the orthodox use the Phylacteries and some the Fringes. None of these symbols is used by members of the reform synagogue.

The point should be stressed that all of these symbols have been prescribed by the Torah so that in each waking hour, no matter where they may be, Jews will be constantly reminded of the presence of God and of their duties to Him.

There is another ceremonial prescribed in the books of Exodus and Numbers, known as the Redemption of the first born. If the first born was a son, he belonged to the service of God. When the members of the tribe of Levites were designated as the assistants to the priests, in place of the first born, the father was required to make a contribution to redeem his son. The ceremonial now consists of a family gathering, usually at the home of the parents, thirty-one days after birth. The child is handed over to a descendant of the priestly class (the Kohanim) who, upon the receipt of some silver money, returns the child to the father. The orthodox Jews continue to observe this ceremonial.

Finally, in their relationship with God, God imposes upon all Jews the requirement of being righteous. The Scriptures tell us that man is created in the image of God. This expression does not have any reference to physical form, as God is incorporeal. It must be taken symbolically. It means that man as a personality has within him the potentiality of developing and exercising those qualities which we attribute to God and to which we refer as Godly. These qualities are largely embraced in the word, righteousness.

This word has been used many times in this book and it is appropriate that its meaning, when used in a religious or ethical sense, should be explained. Righteousness means that which is right, judged by the religious and ethical code given to man by God. Righteousness can be deemed to be the sum total of all goodness; in fact, in a religious and ethical sense, righteousness and goodness are synonymous.

A great rabbi, in a sermon recently delivered before a group of boys and girls who were being confirmed, summed up the requirements of the ethical code by saying that God expected all of us to be good persons. He said that negatively, goodness meant that neither by word nor act would we do anything that would bring distress, pain or unhappiness to another, and that affirmatively, goodness meant that we would at all times practice justice, kindness, humility, honesty, charity and other acts of goodness.

He said that there were two simple tests each of us could apply to ourselves to see whether we were good persons.

He described the first test as the external test. If our acquaintances and friends come to us not alone on light and pleasant occasions when everything is going well with them but also at times when they are troubled and worried, seeking our consolation and our advice, then these persons have felt our goodness and we are good, righteous.

The second test is the internal test. When we believe in justice, kindness, humility, honesty, charity and other acts of goodness, we must ask ourselves whether we are actively and affirmatively conducting ourselves in that manner. For example, if we believe in charity, we must ask ourselves whether we have been charitable, whether we have given charity commensurate with our financial ability and whether we have given charity for charity's own sake and unselfishly. If we believe in justice, we must ask ourselves whether in our relationship with our family, our other kin, our friends and in all our business and social relations, we have been just. If our answers are in the affirmative, then we have been good, righteous.

There have been outlined the requirements of the religious code in man's relationship with God. As has been stated, belief, even though it be completely sincere, is not enough. Jews must do and they must act. They have du-

ties that they must affirmatively and actively perform.
Thus, translating the beliefs into action, we find that the
laws binding upon Jews in their relationship with God
require them to perform five groups of duties:

First—Jews must acknowledge that God is the one
God and that there is no other, they must consecrate
themselves to Him, they must revere him, be grateful to
Him, have trust and faith in Him, love Him, and submit
themselves to His will. Prayer helps to bring about the
realization of these acts and emotions. In the chapter on
PRAYER, there are detailed the nature of prayer and the
proper manner of approach to God in praying.

Second—Jews must observe the Sabbath. This is fully
covered in the chapter on the SABBATH.

Third—Jews must observe the three holidays and the
solemn days enjoined upon them by the Torah. The manner of observance has already been outlined in this chapter.

Fourth—Jews must observe the rite of circumcision
and the symbols to the extent that the branch of the religion to which they adhere, requires them so to do.

Finally—Jews must live righteously. To live righteously is commanded of them by God. It is one of the
most important of the groups of duties that God expects
them to faithfully and fully comply with. They may fail
in some respects with regard to holidays or to symbols,
but they must not fail in any manner in their duties with
respect to righteousness. The meaning of righteousness
has already been discussed. In the next chapter, devoted
to ethical duties, man to man, righteous living in this
relationship will be gone into more fully.

Thus, summarizing the active duties of the Jews toward God, as embodied in the laws, they consist of prayer, the observance of the Sabbath, of the holidays, of the solemn days, of the rite of circumcision, of the symbols to the extent required by the branch of Judaism to which they belong, and of righteous living.

Chapter X

THE LAW—MAN TO MAN

PART of the Fourth Commandment and the remaining six commandments express the duties—man to man.

The Fourth Commandment, that portion which has reference to the relationship of man to man— In it (Sabbath) thou shalt not do any manner of work, thou, nor thy son, nor thy daughter, nor thy man-servant, nor thy maid-servant, nor thy cattle, nor thy stranger that is within thy gates.

The Fifth Commandment—Honor thy father and thy mother, that thy days may be long upon the land which the Lord thy God giveth thee.

The Sixth Commandment—Thou shalt not murder.

The Seventh Commandment—Thou shalt not commit adultery.

The Eighth Commandment—Thou shalt not steal.

The Ninth Commandment—Thou shalt not bear false witness against thy neighbor.

The Tenth Commandment—Thou shalt not covet thy neighbor's house; thou shalt not covet thy neighbor's wife, nor his man-servant, nor his maid-servant, nor his ox, nor his ass, nor anything that is thy neighbor's.

It is appropriate at this point to call attention to the compilations made by scholars at different times, organizing in systematic form the decisions, rules and regulations scattered throughout the Talmud. These compilations include almost every situation that may arise in the relationship of man to man.

The first great work of this character was written by Moses Maimonides in the twelfth century of the present era. These decisions, rules and regulations were separated and organized under specific headings. Maimonides divided them into fourteen divisions or books. So that the reader may appreciate the scope of the subjects covered, a few may be mentioned: Conjugal relationships such as marriage and divorce, forbidden sexual relations, obligations assumed by oaths and vows, cleanness and uncleanness, torts and compensation for damages, transactions involving buying and selling, the relationship of debtors and creditors, the duties of trustees and judicial procedure including the manner of conduct of the trial, the nature and weighing of the evidence and the penalties to be imposed.

About four hundred years later, in the sixteenth century, Joseph Caro made a new codification which was issued under the name of the Schulchan Aruch (set table). This work became the standard on Jewish law, and, to the extent that it can be applied to our present day civilization, has been accepted as such by the orthodox synagogue.

It is not the purpose of this book to list or to even summarize the decisions, rules and regulations contained in this great work. Practically every phase of human life is included and it is amazing how currently applicable are many of the principles set forth in this code. A number of them will be given. In some instances, the rather quaint and archaic wording and expressions of this work have been retained. Readers interested in the contents of the Schulchan Aruch, beyond that given in this book, will find a reading of it very much worthwhile.

The Fourth Commandment embraces the relationship between employer and employee. Although it refers specifically only to the requirement that those who labor shall be afforded an opportunity to rest, there are implied the broader principles of the fair and just treatment of those who labor.

Many of the rules contained in the Schulchan Aruch relating to this subject are no longer necessary in view of social legislation which has become such an important part of the federal and state laws. Our society has become much more alive to the need for social justice. In addition, labor has developed sufficient strength through union organization to insist upon and secure fair conditions of employment.

However, to give the reader an idea of the detail that was gone into in defining the proper relationship between master and servant, we mention some of these rules:

The wages of a hired workman must be paid on the due date before the sun goes down. This regulation is taken directly from the book of Deuteronomy, which also provides that one shall not oppress a hired servant that is poor and needy, whether he be of his brethren, or of strangers that are in the land.

If the employer should not have the funds with which to make payment, it is considered pious conduct for him to borrow the money so that there will be no delay in payment to the employee.

Where a hired workman has spoiled the work, even if such damage has been caused by his negligence, it is considered a religious duty for the master to waive his legal right of reimbursement and to forgive the employee.

There are also rules which require that the workman give effective service to the employer. There is the prohibition against a workman working all night and then hiring himself out by day since, owing to his night work, he becomes unfit to do a good day's work. The workman is also forbidden to starve or to stint himself for he thereby weakens himself and is not able to do the work for his master in a proper manner.

The keynote of the relationship of employer to employee and of employee to employer is that of fairness, equity and justice.

Stated in broad terms, Jews are required by the laws, as set forth in the Schulchan Aruch, to be fair and just in their relationship with their employees; they are admonished to develop a social point of view and strive for social justice; and since all men are equal before God, they are required to promote, within the limits of their ability, equal opportunity for all to earn their livelihood.

The Fifth Commandment requires us to honor our parents and to show them the respect which is their due. Both parents must be equally honored. While in the Fifth

Commandment the father is mentioned first, when this commandment is repeated in the book of Leviticus, the mother is first referred to.

Probably the only utterly true, complete and unselfish love of one person for another is that of a parent for his child. Children should reciprocate and return such love and affection. The minds and hearts of most parents are largely concerned with, bound up with, absorbed in and revolve about their children, their welfare and their happiness.

Parents hunger for the affection of their children. It is not enough that the child has reciprocal love and affection for his parents. Parents should be given the pleasure and joy of concrete evidence of this love and affection. By word, by embrace and by gift children should ever express in outward form their attitude toward those who, as instruments of the Divinity, gave them life and being.

As part of a respectful and obedient attitude toward their parents, children should give consideration and heed to the opinions and advice of their parents.

These acts should be performed by children not only while under the direct care and control of their parents, or while they are still living in their household, but should be continued with the same full sincerity when they have become emancipated, when they have reached maturity and have started independent lives of their own.

If parents need financial help, it is the duty of children to give it and such help should be given not only as a matter of duty, but also in a loving, generous and willing spirit.

The Schulchan Aruch states that three partners share
in man's creation: One's father, one's mother and the Almighty. The father and mother create the physical body
and the Almighty breathes life into the body and endows
it with a soul, a part of Himself, resident therein. Thus,
since God participated with our parents, jointly, in our
creation, when we honor our parents, God himself is also
honored.

Some of the regulations prescribed in the Schulchan
Aruch bearing on the relationship between parents and
children are herewith given:

A son must stand in the presence of his mother and
father.

Even if his father be wicked and a sinner, it is proper
for the son to honor him.

From the book of Exodus comes the law that he that
smiteth his father or his mother, or he that curseth his
father or mother, shall surely be put to death.

Whosoever shall put his father or mother to shame,
though only by word or hint, he is included among those
whom God will punish.

On the other hand, a parent is forbidden to place an
unduly heavy yoke upon his children.

A parent must not be unreasonably exacting in matters relating to his honor, and thereby cause his children
to stumble.

A parent should rather overlook, be patient with and
forgive his children's shortcomings.

The Sixth Commandment prohibits murder. The life and soul resident in our body are the most precious gifts of God. Thus the taking of life without full and complete justification and without full legal sanction and not according to law, is the most grievous offense that can be committed not only against society but as well against God. He who commits murder places himself outside the pale of society and the bounds of God's protection and his punishment must fit the crime.

The Torah places special safeguards around the person accused of murder to assure him a fair trial. In the book of Numbers it is provided that the accused shall be permitted to reside in certain specified localities, cities of refuge, until after he has been duly tried, in order to guard against attack by any avenger; that the accused may be adjudged guilty only after a fair trial at which testimony has been given against him by several witnesses, the testimony of a single witness being insufficient to support a verdict of guilty.

A person who has been found guilty of murder may not expiate his crime by any money payment, but must suffer the penalty of death. It is provided in the book of Deuteronomy that a father shall not be put to death for the crime of his child, nor a child for that of his father, each person to pay the penalty for the proven guilt of his own crime only.

Kidnapping is placed in the same category as murder and the penalty of death is imposed upon the convicted person. In the book of Exodus it is stated that he that stealeth a man and selleth him, or if he be found in his hand, he shall surely be put to death. There is a similar law in the book of Deuteronomy.

The Seventh Commandment forbids us to commit adultery.

From the earliest times the foundation of society and the hub of civilization have been the family. Without the unit of the family we could not have an orderly or civilized society. Therefore, adultery strikes at the very heart of society. Idolatry, murder and adultery were grouped together as the most heinous crimes, never to be committed under any circumstances, even if refusal be at the sacrifice of life itself.

The Jew has always been jealous of the sanctity and the purity of his marital relations and of his home. The wife is obligated to comport herself in such manner as to avoid even the possibility of suspicion of any improprieties in her conduct.

Up to about the time of the destruction of the Second Temple, in the first century of the present era, a husband who merely suspected his wife of wrongdoing had the right to require her to undergo the "ordeal of the bitter waters." This followed the procedure prescribed in the book of Numbers. The ordeal was conducted at the Temple. It included a thorough questioning by the priests. The theory was that if guilty, the effect of the examination and of the entire ceremonial would be a confession.

The laws of the Torah relating to personal purity are strict and exacting. The following are the more important ones:

If a woman commits adultery, both persons participating in the adulterous act are subject to the penalty of death. In the book of Deuteronomy, it is provided that if a man be found lying with a woman married to a husband, they shall both die, the man that lay with the woman and the woman.

If any man take a wife, and say "I took this woman and I found not in her the tokens of virginity," then shall her father take and bring forth the tokens of the damsel's virginity unto the elders of the city. If this thing be true, then shall they bring out the damsel to the door of her father's house, and the men of the city shall stone her so that she die; because she hath wrought a wanton deed in Israel, to play the harlot in her father's house.

If there be a damsel that is a virgin betrothed unto a man, and a man find her in the city, and lie with her; then both of them shall be brought unto the gate of that city and both shall be stoned to death. But if the man find the damsel that is betrothed in the field, and the man take hold of her and lie with her; then the man only that lay with her shall die. But unto the damsel nothing shall be done, for he found her in the field and there was none to save her.

If a man find a damsel that is a virgin, that is not betrothed, and lay hold on her and lie with her, and they be found, she shall be his wife, because he has humbled her; he may not put her away (divorce) all his days.

A man shall not lie carnally with his neighbor's wife, to defile himself with her.

Profane not thy daughter, to make her a harlot, lest the land fall into harlotry, and the land become full of lewdness.

There shall be no harlot of the daughters of Israel, neither shall there be a sodomite of the sons of Israel.

Man shall not lie with mankind, as woman with womankind; it is abomination.

A woman shall not wear that which pertaineth unto a man, neither shall a man put on a woman's garment; for whosoever doeth these things is an abomination unto the Lord.

The Torah also defines those relationships which are considered incestuous and are therefore forbidden.

Some of the laws contained in the Schulchan Aruch relating to the marital status are:

Each male is required to marry and it is his duty to propagate. He fulfills this duty by having a son and daughter.

In seeking a wife a man should endeavor to take as his bride a woman possessing modesty, kindliness and charitableness.

Marriage is forbidden where the primary consideration is money or other personal advantage.

During the first year of married life, the husband is freed from military duty and he may not be called upon to engage in any enterprise; so that he may live happily at home with his wife. This law is taken directly from the book of Deuteronomy. The custom of freeing the husband from the duty of engaging in private enterprise has been observed even in modern times, particularly in the case of a student. This custom was commonly practiced by many orthodox Jews in Europe until about fifty years ago. Board, lodging and other needs were provided by the bride's parents for the young couple, usually at the bride's parents' home.

A husband is enjoined to treat his wife with respect and consideration, for it is because of his wife that his house is blessed.

A husband must be careful not to wound his wife's feelings through words, for a woman is soft-hearted and weeps over a trifle. The Lord heeds tears, for the gates of tears are never locked.

Chapter XI

THE LAW—MAN TO MAN

THE Eighth Commandment prohibits stealing. This commandment is intended to impose the highest degree of integrity and honor in our business, commercial and property relationships. It covers not only outright theft but any sharp or unfair practices which may result in the unjust enrichment of one at the expense of or to the detriment of his fellow man.

Any financial advantage secured by short weight or measurement, by cheating, by embezzlement, by fraud, by forgery, by receiving or dealing in stolen goods, by misrepresentation, by taking advantage of the lack of knowledge, information or experience of others, each, in a broad sense constitutes a violation of the Eighth Commandment. Honesty and fair dealing are required to be the keynote of all our business, commercial and financial relationships.

Included among the laws prescribed in the Torah relating to honesty and fair dealing are the following:

Ye shall not steal; neither shalt ye deal falsely, nor lie one to another. Thou shalt not defraud thy neighbor nor rob him.

If a man deliver unto his neighbor money or stuff to

keep, and it be stolen out of the neighbor's house; if the thief be caught, he shall pay double. If the thief be not caught, then the neighbor shall come near unto God (attend the sanctuary) so that inquiry may be made whether he, himself, has not laid his hands unto such goods. He whom God shall condemn (who is found guilty) shall pay double.

And if thou sell aught unto thy neighbor or buy of thy neighbor's land, ye shall not wrong one another.

Ye shall do no unrighteousness in judgment, in mete-yard, in weight, or in measure. Thou shalt not have in thy bag diverse weights, a great and a small. Thou shalt not have in thy house diverse measures, a great and a small.

Thou shalt not see thy brother's ox or his sheep driven away (going astray), and hide thyself from them (refuse to help him); thou shalt surely bring them back unto thy brother. And if thy brother be not nigh unto thee (does not dwell nearby), and thou know him not, then shalt thou bring it to thy house, and it shall be with thee until thy brother require it, and thou shalt restore it to him. And so shalt thou do with his ass, and so shalt thou do with his garment, and so shalt thou do with every lost thing of thy brother's, which thou hast found.

The Schulchan Aruch is replete with laws defining these relationships:

As to Stolen Property

It is forbidden to take anything without permission from one's neighbor, even with the intention of returning it, and even if the taking has been merely in jest or to annoy him.

The thief must return the very thing that was stolen. Restitution in money is not enough.

If the stolen article has been lost or altered so that it cannot be restored to its original state, then and only then may restitution be made by the payment of a sum of money equivalent to the value of the stolen article.

It is forbidden to derive the slightest benefit from stolen property.

The poor may not accept from a thief any money or goods as charity.

One may not derive benefit from anything belonging to one's neighbor without his knowledge and consent.

As to Property Damage

We may not wilfully, deliberately or carelessly damage the property of our neighbor even with the intention of making restitution.

One is forbidden to do anything on his own premises whereby his neighbor will sustain damage.

One who sustains damage may not rid himself thereof if by so doing he shall cause his neighbor damage, as, for example, causing water to flow off his land and onto that of his neighbor.

If the king's army should come to town, and the townsmen be required to billet the soldiers, it is forbidden for one of the townsmen to bribe the commander to exempt him, for he is thereby causing damage to another townsman.

As to Litigation

When there is a controversy between two persons they should in good faith attempt peacefully to compromise, each making the other some allowance in order to avoid the institution of legal proceedings.

Occasionally litigants choose men to arbitrate apart from the law courts. This is a proper course to pursue and the verdict will be properly effectuated provided the arbitration is conducted in a just manner.

When one owes money and is able to repay, he is forbidden to seek means of avoiding repayment or of compelling the creditor to accept less, by making collection difficult.

One may not present a false plea regardless of the fact that, although innocent, if he pleads truthfully judgment will be given against him.

A litigant is forbidden to present his case before the judge unless the opposite party to the litigation is given the opportunity of being present.

In the same manner that the judge who takes a bribe transgresses a negative precept contained in the book of Leviticus, so he who gives the bribe transgresses this negative precept.

One who can testify on behalf of his neighbor must do so, truthfully. If he suppresses his testimony, he is guilty according to the laws of the Torah.

The testimony of one, induced to testify by a promise of reward, is null and void.

To serve as judges, men possessing the following qualifications shall be selected: Wisdom in the Torah, humility, reverence, hate of money, love of truth, love of them by their fellow men and possession of a good reputation.

As to the Sale of Property

Whether it is the seller or the buyer who deceives, it is a transgression of the prohibitory law contained in the book of Leviticus.

If one has something to sell, it is forbidden to make it look better than it really is in order thereby to deceive the buyer.

It is forbidden to mix bad food with good food and to sell the product as good food, or to mix inferior liquor with superior liquor.

It is required to measure and to weigh with a generous eye.

If one has agreed to buy or rent property at a specified price, whether it be real property or chattels, and before the transaction is completed the buyer is forestalled by some other person, who knows of the agreement, the latter is to be deemed a wicked person.

If one desires to acquire his neighbor's house or other property and his neighbor is not willing to sell it, he must not seek to overcome his neighbor's will by bringing pressure to bear upon him through threats, the influence of his friends or in any other manner.

The Ninth Commandment prohibits the bearing of false witness against our neighbor. This commandment embraces in its broader sense the concept of doing justice at all times. We are unjust not only when we bear false witness but also when we lie, when we carry tales, when we deliberately color the facts, when we do not give a person the benefit of a doubt.

The test of justice is that we shall do unto others as we would have them do unto us. This commandment in its broad aspects embraces justice in every relationship we may have with other members of the human family.

As previously explained, righteousness is the sum total of goodness, and the measure of our right behavior toward our fellow man is the extent to which we are righteous in all our associations with him.

It is interesting to observe that notwithstanding the all-inclusiveness of the word righteousness, the Torah stresses justice and there is often coupled in the Torah the word justice with that of righteousness. Although doing justice is doing right and thus related to and included and embraced within righteousness, justice is conceived in Judaism as of such paramount importance that it is nevertheless separately stated.

Moreover, in the Scriptures, justice has, in several instances, been placed ahead of the word righteousness. The reference is often "justice and righteousness." This is no mere coincidence. It was done deliberately and advisedly to stress and to stress again the transcendent importance of doing justice.

Courts of justice are considered sacred. When speaking of attending a court of justice, the Torah uses the expression of coming to God, of standing before the Lord. If the Jews had been limited to giving to the world a single ethical principle, they would have undoubtedly selected justice; and of the many eternal contributions Judaism has made to civilization, perhaps the greatest has been its concept of justice.

Some of the laws contained in the Torah having direct reference to justice are:

Judges and officers shalt thou make thee in all thy gates and they shall judge the people with righteous judgment. Thou shalt not wrest (tamper with) judgment; thou shalt not respect (be partial to) persons; neither shalt thou take a gift (bribe); for a gift doth blind the eyes of the wise, and pervert the words of the righteous. Justice, justice, shalt thou follow.

You shall hear the causes between your brethren, and judge righteously between a man and his brother, and the stranger that is with him. Ye shall hear the small and the great alike; ye shall not be afraid of the face of any man; for the judgment is God's.

Thou shalt not utter a false report (repeat a baseless rumor); put not thine hand with the wicked to be an unrighteous witness. Thou shalt not follow a multitude to do evil; neither shalt thou bear witness in a cause, to turn aside after a multitude to pervert justice (to side with an unjust majority).

A single witness shall not rise up against a man for any iniquity (crime), or for any sin. At the mouth of two witnesses, or at the mouth of three witnesses shall a matter be established. If an unrighteous witness appear against any man to bear perverted witness against him; then both men between whom there is the controversy, shall stand before the Lord (namely), before the priests and judges. And the judges shall inquire diligently; and, if the witness hath testified falsely against his brother, then shall ye do unto him as he had purposed to do unto his brother; so shalt thou put away evil from the midst of thee.

Keep thee far from (avoid) false charges; and the innocent and righteous (guiltless) slay thou not; for I will not justify (will not acquit) the wicked.

In the Talmud, where each duty of daily life has been worked out in the greatest detail—the principle of justice has been given the closest and the greatest attention and has been most emphasized. It is apparent from the illustrations already given in the earlier part of this, and in the previous chapter, of rules and regulations contained in the Schulchan Aruch, that justice is the goal always sought. No man may fairly call himself a good Jew if he does not practice justice in both his private and public life.

The Tenth Commandment which prohibits covetousness, in a broad sense prohibits each type of wrongful doing which in effect is the cause of the wrongs prohibited under Commandments Six to Nine, inclusive. When we covet, we place ourselves in a frame of mind which, if not restrained, may result in the commission of any of these crimes.

The purpose of this commandment is to enjoin upon us the use of self-restraint in our desires. One must not covet; one must not seek after those things to which he is not entitled. We are instructed by this commandment not to be envious or selfish or to bear malice.

We have the right to legitimate and proper ambitions and the right to strive to attain them in an ethical and lawful manner—to possess a home as good as our neighbor's, to have a wife as desirable as his and to have assets similar to or equal in value to those of our neighbor. But when we covet and seek those things that belong to our neighbor, then we may be tempted to commit murder, adultery, theft and injustice in order to secure them, and this commandment is intended to keep us from doing so.

Chapter XII

THE LAW—MAN TO MAN

THERE are a group of ethical duties which are not directly deducible from those imposed by the Ten Commandments which head Chapter X, but which come within their broad interpretation. Most of them are specifically mentioned in the Torah and all of them are embraced in the Talmud and are contained in the Schulchan Aruch.

The first of these is charity. The code specifies two different kinds of charity. One kind is that which is ordinarily intended when the word, charity, is used, namely, that of giving alms, of giving money or goods to the poor. This is not an act regarded as one entitling the giver to special commendation. Jews regard such deeds as mandatory upon those who have worldly goods. Those that have, must share part of their means with those who are less fortunate than themselves and in need.

The second form of charity has reference not so much to material help as to that aid and comfort which are given through consolation, advice and companionship. It is the kind of charitable act we perform when we attend a house of mourning and by our presence mitigate the sorrow, sadness and tragedy which have come to the bereaved. It is the kind of act we perform when we visit the sick and by friendly conversation and real solicitude for his recovery, give comfort and hope to the ailing. It is the help we give when we lend moral support to the extension of aid to widows and orphans. It is the help we give when we furnish guidance and protection to the young, the aged, the weak, the blind, the crippled and the stranger in our midst. Also included among these acts is the burial of the dead. This last mentioned deed is considered especially worthy because it is performed with the purest of motives.

While the first form of charity has reference to persons who have the financial ability to give, the second applies to rich and poor alike and must be practiced by every individual. There is no word in the Hebrew language which is the exact equivalent of our word "charity." To give charity is to be righteous. It is interesting to note that the first form of charity is embraced in the Hebrew word, Zedakah, which means righteousness, goodness. The second type of charity is embraced in the Hebrew words, Gemilut Hesed, which may be interpreted to mean the bestowal of loving kindness.

In the books of Leviticus and Deuteronomy, it is provided that when the harvest shall be reaped, the corners of the field, the gleanings of the harvest and of the vineyard, the forgotten sheaf, the fallen fruit and the fruit remaining on the boughs of the olive tree, are to be set aside for the stranger, the fatherless, for the widow and for the poor. The Torah stresses that the hands of every individual shall be opened wide to the poor and needy brother of the land.

There are a number of interesting and instructive regulations in the Schulchan Aruch relating to charity, some of which are:

Every man must contribute to charity, according to his means. Even if one can give but little, yet he should not abstain from giving—for the little he gives is equally worthy with the large contribution of the rich.

When one gives, he must give freely and everything must be of the best. When he feeds the hungry, he must feed them with the best from his table and when he clothes the naked he must clothe them with his best garments.

He who gives alms to the poor with an unfriendly mien and downcast face, even if he give a thousand pieces of gold, there is no merit in his giving; for he has marred it by his manner of giving and he transgresses.

It is forbidden to turn away, empty-handed, the poor who begs, even if he is given only one dried fig.

It is forbidden to rebuke a poor man or to raise an angry voice against him, for his heart is already crushed and humble. Woe unto him who has put the poor to shame.

A promise to give charity is in the nature of a vow.

The highest degree of charity is attained by him who, by making a loan to an impoverished person, or by entering into a partnership with him or by obtaining some business or employment for him, helps him to become self-supporting.

No man should boast of the charitable contributions he makes.

It is advisable to make charitable contributions in secrecy as much as possible.

One should at all times suffer hardship rather than become dependent on man.

He who has no need of taking charity, yet deceives people and does take it, will become dependent on charity before he dies.

There is a negative commandment against the taking of interest. Interest on loans, no matter how indirectly collected, whether in money or kind, is prohibited. The prohibition applied only in the case where the borrower was an Israelite and did not apply to strangers.

This exception appears odd and surprising in view of the solicitude, under the laws, for the care and protection of the stranger. The stranger is even placed in the same category as the widow and orphan. An explanation that has been given is that the exception was provided to benefit the stranger, not to harm him. If no interest could be charged, it would be natural for an Israelite to refuse a loan to a stranger. The stranger did not necessarily have his roots in the land as in the case of a native. He might leave the country and thus prevent the lender from enforcing repayment. Accordingly, to encourage Israelites to make loans to strangers who might be in need of them, there was permitted the incentive of charging interest.

In some translations of the Scriptures, the word "usury" is used instead of "interest." When so used, usury does not have its present colloquial meaning—a charge in excess of the maximum rates permitted by law. It means interest—any charge made for the loan of money or goods.

Some of the laws of the Torah, relating to loans, pledges and interest, are herewith given:

When thou dost lend thy neighbor any manner of loan, thou shalt not go into his house to fetch his pledge. Thou shalt stand without, and the man to whom thou dost lend shall bring forth the pledge without unto thee.

If thou at all take thy neighbor's garment to pledge, thou shalt restore it unto him by that the sun goeth down; for that is his only covering, it is his garment for his skin.

No man shall take the nether or the upper millstone to pledge; for he taketh a man's life to pledge.

Thou shalt not lend upon interest to thy brother: interest of money, interest of victuals, interest of anything that is lent upon interest.

These laws prohibiting the charge of interest had reference to a period when loans were made primarily to those in need. These requirements, relating to the needy, hold good and are binding today.

However, radical changes have taken place in our industrial and commercial life. Moneys are loaned to finance business enterprises, to provide for their operation, for their expansion and for other manifold purposes, and the laws against charging interest are not applicable to these situations. Thus it is entirely ethical to finance these operations for compensation. Money and credits in these instances are the equivalent of goods and wares. Money is a commodity to be used and compensated for, like any other commodity. So, when money is used in the manner of a commodity, interest may be charged. But where a loan is made, in money or in kind, to the needy individual, the charge of interest is prohibited.

Another requirement which the laws impose is mercy. Each person must be merciful to his fellow man. He must be understanding. He must realize that being human is to be frail and weak and subject to all the temptations of the flesh.

He is also instructed to be gentle and merciful with animals. In the book of Deuteronomy it is provided that an ox and an ass shall not be joined together in plowing. Since they are of unequal strength, the weaker will be unable to keep up with the stronger and thus will suffer. There is another law that the ox shall not be muzzled when he treads out the corn, since it would be cruel to have him desire to eat and be prevented by the muzzle.

The aged must be respected and honored. In the book of Leviticus it is stated that we shall rise before the hoary head and honor the face of the old man.

Kindliness and unselfishness are also virtues which are separately enumerated as rules of conduct in man's association with his fellow man.

In the book of Deuteronomy there is the requirement: If there be among us a needy man, one of our brethren, within any of our gates, in our land, we shall not harden our heart, nor shut our hand from our needy brother; but we shall surely open our hand unto him. We shall surely give unto him, and our heart shall not be grieved when we give unto him; because for this thing the Lord, our God, will bless us in all our work, and in all that we put our hand unto. For the poor shall never cease out of the land.

There is a similar law in the book of Leviticus: If thy brother be waxen poor, and his means fail with thee, then thou shalt uphold him; as a stranger and a settler shall he live with thee.

The laws are especially solicitous of the welfare of the widow, the orphan, the deaf and the blind.

The widow and the orphan are the special wards of God. In the book of Exodus it is provided: Ye shall not afflict any widow or fatherless child. If thou afflict them in any wise, if they cry unto Me, I shall surely hear their cry, and my wrath shall wax hot; and in the book of Deuteronomy: He doth execute justice for the fatherless and widow.

In the book of Leviticus, it is stated: Thou shalt not curse the deaf, nor put a stumblingblock before the blind.

As to unselfishness—self interest is not only necessary but laudable. Unless we have and pursue the normal urge of self-development and self-advancement, we shall fail in our duty to ourselves, our families and to society. When, however, we carry our self-interest to the point where we think only of and provide solely for ourselves, we commit the sin of selfishness. This thought is well expressed by the great rabbi Hillel: If I am not for myself, who will be for me, and if I am only for myself, what am I?

To be forgiving means to follow in the footsteps of God. As God forgives us for our sins when we truly repent, so must we follow this Godly trait in our relationship with our fellow man. We must develop a forgiving point of view and we must practice this Godly trait and always keep before us the maxim that: to err is human; to forgive, divine.

Truthfulness is enjoined upon every individual. Falsehood, deception and hypocrisy, no matter in what form and no matter what the motive, are forbidden.

There are several interesting regulations in the Schulchan Aruch relating to deceptive and malicious statements:

It is forbidden to deceive even where no loss can result therefrom.

When one expresses something with his tongue and does not mean it, as when one seemingly passes honor to his neighbor, which is not his real intention, such conduct is forbidden.

One should always let the mouth and heart correspond, thereby cultivating truth, uprightness and purity of heart.

War has been the bedfellow of mankind from the dawn of civilization. Probably in no country has any generation of its inhabitants escaped war in one form or another—wars of conquest, wars of defense, internal revolutions or rebellions. War has become so commonplace in the scheme of things that it has even been said that wars are God's will, to reduce the ever-swelling population of the earth. No more wicked or untrue statement has ever been made. Wars have been caused not by any design of God but because of man's persistence in disregarding the religious and ethical code given to him.

All the great modern religions warn against war and urge peace. More than any other, Judaism is a religion of peace. There is scarcely a prayer in its prayer books that does not recite or end with a fervent plea to God for peace (Shalom). Special reference is made in the laws to the man who is a lover of peace. He is called a man of God. Judaism most solemnly enjoins each of its followers to develop a peace-loving disposition and to practice peace in his personal and social relations. Shalom is the keynote of man in his relationship to his fellow man. And it is the keynote of man organized in the form of government.

Judaism teaches loyalty and devotion to the government of the country in which its adherents are resident. The code speaks of the individual's duty to the king of the land in which he resides. The king, of course, represents sovereignty and where there is a republican form of government, loyalty, patriotism and devotion are to the state. Jews are specifically instructed to pray to God for the welfare of the state and they are required to abide by and comply with the laws of their country.

The Jews are a people, an eternal people, united by language, a common history, customs and ceremonials, by a great religion of the one living and loving God, and by a common destiny. Each Jew owes full, complete and unswerving loyalty to his people. It is mandatory upon each Jew to help his people, not alone with goods and money but by personal and public association and identification with his fellow co-religionists in all matters relating to their religious, ethical, social, financial and personal welfare.

The distress of the Jews in Poland is the distress of all Jews; the persecution of the Jews in any country is the persecution of the Jews of every other country; they are brethren. The code imposes upon each Jew the solemn duty of never permitting to go unheeded the cry for help of his fellow Jews, from whatever part of the world it may come. Each Jew is in duty bound to give succor to the oppressed of his people, as if they were members of his own household.

If any one phrase were to be used to cover the broad implications of the commandments enumerated in these chapters relating to THE LAW—MAN TO MAN, it would be: Love thy neighbor as thyself. This phrase has not only been used in the Torah as a law, but it has also been used, time and again, in the commentaries of the great scholars and rabbis.

This phrase has reference not alone to Jews but—to all mankind. In the books of Exodus, Leviticus and Deuteronomy, it is expressly provided that the Jews shall not

wrong the stranger or oppress him, that they shall love
the stranger as they love themselves, and they are reminded in this connection that they, themselves, were
once strangers in the land of Egypt.

In the book of Exodus it is stated: A stranger shalt thou
not wrong, neither shalt thou oppress him; for ye were
strangers in the land of Egypt. It is expressed in the book
of Leviticus: The stranger that sojourneth with you shall
be unto you as the home-born among you, and thou shalt
love him as thyself; for ye were strangers in the land of
Egypt. And in the book of Deuteronomy this commandment is given in the following words: Love thee therefore
the stranger; for ye were strangers in the land of Egypt.

Whenever in the past the Jew sought to decide whether
his conduct toward his fellow man was righteous, he applied the test embraced in this law whether he loved his
neighbor as himself. The Jew of today may test himself
similarly and if his conduct is consistent with this principle, then he may be assured that he is acting righteously
and since righteousness is Godliness, that he is acting in
a Godly manner.

Thus—summing up—the laws in the relationship of
man to man embrace and require of the Jew: Social justice, fairness and equity in all dealings between employee
and employer—respect, honor and love of parents—recognition of the sacredness of life—purity in marital relationship and in home life and also personal purity—honesty and fair dealings in all business, commercial and
financial association—justice in private and public rela-

tionship—freedom from covetousness, envy, selfishness and malice—charity, both Zedakah and Gemilut Hesed —the making of loans, in money or in kind to the needy, free from any interest charge direct or indirect—mercy and gentleness, both to his fellow man and to animals— respect and honor for the aged—kindliness and unselfishness, especially toward the widow, the orphan, the stranger, the deaf and the blind—forgiveness—truthfulness—peace and peace lovingness, in personal, social and public relationship—loyalty and devotion to his country —loyalty and devotion to his people, no matter where they dwell—and finally, summarizing all these laws in the commandment: Love thy neighbor as thyself.

Chapter XIII

THE LAW—MAN TO HIMSELF

No ONE of the Ten Commandments in and of itself has direct reference solely to man in relationship to himself. The Torah, however, includes among its six hundred and thirteen commandments many laws which so apply, and many decisions and rules, based on these laws, have been listed in the Schulchan Aruch.

Pursuing the policy outlined in the prior chapters, of not being confined to the specific precepts enunciated in the Ten Commandments, but of reading into them the laws which can be deemed in a broad way to be derived from them, there are set forth in this chapter the more important of the laws dealing with the individual, in relationship to himself.

It is self-evident that if a person is to have the ability, willingness and desire to fulfill and comply with the laws, he must have the physical, mental and ethical equipment necessary to carry them out.

The laws designated for observance by each individual are not given for the selfish benefit of the individual alone. The code makes it clear that God has in mind all mankind. The greater goal sought in having each person perfect himself, physically, mentally and ethically, is to enable him more effectively to serve his fellow man, for the greater benefit of all mankind.

In considering those laws that have reference to his physical well-being, the individual must always keep before him the concept, repeated in different expressions in the Scriptures, that his body is a holy structure, a house of God. In it dwells the soul, part of the Divinity. As he would not profane or desecrate the synagogue, so should he not profane or desecrate his body. In order for him to maintain his body in a healthy condition, thus enabling him to carry out the other commands of God, there are embraced in the religious and ethical code, dietary and sanitary laws.

These laws consist chiefly of rules relating to personal hygiene, cleanliness and health, and to sanitary conditions. Although personal hygiene and sanitation were known to other peoples, their application was limited to a few, the wealthy and the influential. Among the Jews, the observance of dietary and sanitary laws was part of their religious duties and these laws were generally complied with. At a time when the nature of the functioning of the body was largely unknown, and disease was common, especially leprosy in the Near East, the Jew alone fully realized the absolute necessity of cleanliness, temperate living and the control of physical appetites.

If the Jews were to make their contribution to mankind and fulfill their mission, they could do so only if they survived. Their survival was in jeopardy if they could not keep and maintain a healthy body and a healthy community. Thus there was included in the code a group of rules which had for its purpose the preservation of a healthy body and community. In the same manner that the code made provision for their spiritual conduct and

for their ethical behavior, so also rules were laid down
for their physical welfare.

As to food—the code forbids the eating of certain foods.
Roughly speaking, the proscribed foods consist of the
flesh of such mammals and portions of mammals as are
considered unclean. Only such cattle and beasts can be
eaten as are cloven-footed and chew the cud. As to birds,
some are listed as forbidden food, but no general rule is
laid down. Accordingly, orthodox Jews eat the flesh of
only such birds as are traditionally considered clean. With
respect to fish, all those that have scales and fins are clean
and may be eaten. The eating of shellfish is thus forbidden. All winged animals that creep, with several excep-
tions, are unclean and the eating of the flesh of any creep-
ing thing is forbidden. The rules also apply to the manner of slaughter of animals, and to the condition of the
animal before its slaughter. There is a prohibition against
the eating of the blood of beasts and birds and also against
the mixing of meat and milk.

These dietary laws, in addition to providing for physical well-being, also exercise great influence over the individual in promoting self-restraint. When he learns to control his appetites and his desire for indulgence in foods
which may be attractive to his palate, he helps to attain
greater control, discipline and mastery over himself.

Rules are laid down for personal hygiene and cleanliness. The washing of the hands before the commencement of each meal, periodical bathing, the manner of
washing and bathing, all are set forth in detail. The rules
are especially detailed as to women. Women are pro-
tected by a series of prohibitions imposed upon the male

in order that their physical well-being will be safe-guarded in sexual relations.

The cleanliness of the home, the community and of the house of worship are all provided for.

Rules and regulations were worked out with regard to all phases of life, including birth, marital relations, sex relations and death.

The Talmud contains detailed regulations covering each and every one of these phases—all of which have been collated and grouped in the Schulchan Aruch.

These regulations provide when the individual shall rise, when he shall sleep, when he shall eat, the nature and the amount of food he shall take, when he shall wash, when he shall bathe, what constitute clean and unclean foods, the wholesome and the unwholesome ones, the nature and amount of exercise he shall take. He is cautioned to protect his eyes from too much strain. He is informed of the effect on his health of emotions—joy, grief, anger and fright. He is advised to cultivate good spirits and be joyous to a moderate extent. He is advised not to eat when he is angry, frightened or grieved.

There are regulations for avoiding physical danger. For example, an individual is forbidden from walking in a dangerous place such as near a bulging wall or on a broken bridge. He is forbidden from crossing a stream when the water is rising if it reaches above his loins, as he may be in danger of being swept away by the water. He is forbidden to drink from rivers and also from placing his mouth under a jet of water, lest he sip something harmful. He is forbidden to partake of any food or bever-age out of unclean vessels, or when his hands are unclean.

There are regulations concerning physical injury to himself and the requirement to help a neighbor in danger. One is forbidden to smite his fellow man. If, however, he cannot save himself or his neighbor from the hands of the striker except by striking back, then he is permitted to do so. When one sees his neighbor in distress, it is his duty to make every effort to save him or to employ others to do so.

One of the chief reasons for the survival of the Jews through the ages has been their strict compliance with these laws. During the dark ages, when the black plague and other epidemic diseases were rampant, taking the lives of millions of people in Europe and almost depopulating entire countries, the Jews alone were little affected. In fact, the Jews were accused of having brought about these plagues and of having been immune to them solely by reason of magic. The truth of the matter is that strict observance by the Jews of the dietary and sanitary laws saved them from the ravages of these dreadful calamities.

Those belonging to the orthodox division of the faith and many Jews of the conservative branch generally adhere to and comply with these laws, particularly the dietary laws, but the members of the reform synagogue do not.

As previously stated in this chapter, each individual must also properly equip himself mentally to carry out the laws. There are two general broad divisions of education.

The first has reference to knowledge that is acquired

generally for useful, utilitarian purposes. Such is the knowledge that enables us to be a successful farmer, a competent carpenter, an efficient tradesman, an able and painstaking physician. This type of knowledge enables us to earn our livelihood by constructive work for the support of ourselves, our families and others dependent upon us.

The second kind of education is not utilitarian in purpose. It is knowledge of the past, its history and manner of life, of our contemporary period and also knowledge of the arts and sciences generally. It is knowledge which enables us to take a broader view of life and which helps us to understand our individual relationship and that of our country to the general scheme of things. This form of knowledge is known as culture.

In thinking of all humanity as a partnership, we cannot make our fair contribution to the partnership unless we have developed our mental equipment through these two forms of education. It will be noted that with respect to the so-called useful part of our education, we have applied the adjectives: successful, competent, efficient and painstaking. It is not enough to secure education. We must absorb it so well that we in turn shall be able to contribute to the partnership the maximum of which our mental equipment is capable.

The ethics of Judaism emphasize this—the duty of each to obtain this dual education. Throughout the code it is stressed that the man of education shall be honored. When seeking a husband for their daughter, parents are urged to select not a man of wealth but one of education, and this principle was followed through the ages.

Time and again a man's worth was tested, not by his worldly goods but by his education. It is interesting to note that until recent years, rabbis were not of a professional class, devoted exclusively to their duties as such. They were carpenters, tailors and craftsmen engaged in various other occupations. They became rabbis solely because of their love and devotion for the law and education. No man made his livelihood as a rabbi—that was a labor of love.

Some of the greatest of the Jewish scholars through the centuries, men who had an unquenchable thirst for knowledge, were unconnected with any priesthood. Probably the greatest Jewish scholar since the destruction of the Second Temple and the final dispersion of the Jews, was Moses Maimonides. Maimonides was also the greatest physician of his time. He was the personal physician to Al Afdal, the all-powerful vizier of Saladin, the Sultan of Egypt, who, in the twelfth century, ruled a large part of the Near East. In addition, Maimonides maintained a clinic for many years, to which sick persons flocked from many parts of the then civilized world. Yet he found the time to prepare the first codified version of the Talmud, a mountainous undertaking to which he devoted more than ten years of his life. Other Jewish scholars during the middle ages and in modern times were outstanding physicians and scientists.

Since the time of the dispersion, illiteracy has been almost unknown among the Jews, particularly among its male members. There was a direct responsibility imposed upon the father to train his children to fulfill the laws of the Torah and the rules and regulations prescribed by the Talmud. He was obligated to commence his son's education of the Torah when the child began to talk and to employ a teacher for him as soon as he was strong enough to attend school, often before he was four years of age. At the age of five, the child began the study of the Scriptures and at ten, the study of the Talmud. By the time he attained the age of religious responsibility, thirteen, and was formally inducted as a member of the synagogue and the community, in the Bar Mitzvah ceremony, he could read and write Hebrew fluently.

At a time when, throughout the western world, illiteracy was common and knowledge of reading and writing was rare, the Jews were literate.

Chapter XIV

THE LAW—MAN TO HIMSELF

FINALLY, the laws in the relationship of man to himself make it mandatory that each person shall equip himself ethically to enable him to carry out the spirit of God's laws. This imposes on each the duty of reading and studying the Scriptures, for how can the individual comply with the religious and ethical code if he does not know what it contains?

The Scriptures, including the laws, must not only be read, but re-read and studied so that their true meaning and purpose will become as much a part of oneself as his knowledge of reading, writing and arithmetic. Not only the Written Law but the Oral Law, as well, must be read and studied. The religious and ethical code of which there are several summaries and abridged versions in English, should be part of every personal library in addition to the Scriptures, and this code and other religious and ethical writings should be included in regular reading and study.

The habit of devoting oneself to this reading and study at regular intervals must be cultivated, although the amount of time so devoted on each occasion be brief. If it is only one hour each week, the results will be surprisingly great and most gratifying. By so doing, the individual will not only enrich himself with knowledge, but, in addition, he will find that by the periodical return of his thoughts to the Scriptures and to the laws, they will become a part of his personality and will influence for good his actions in his daily contact with his fellow man.

Each individual must learn self-respect. He must hold his own personality in respect. He must have self-confidence. Without assurance in himself, he cannot inspire others to work well for him or with him. It must be self-confidence based upon knowledge, not upon conceit, arrogance, haughtiness or false pride.

We come now to the qualities of humility and modesty, which are stressed in the Scriptures. Humility means a true appreciation of one's personality, a true appraisal of one's strength and at the same time a complete understanding of one's weaknesses. Expressed negatively, it means an absence of self-importance and self-righteousness. We must be humble, we must be contrite in spirit and we must be modest. We are all children of the one God and every other person is as important in God's eyes as we are.

That we are all equal before God, that neither God nor nature draws any line of distinction among human beings, whether as individuals, or as members of the same nation, the same race or the same religion, is evidenced by the fact that neither germs nor disease, nor even death, recognize any such distinctions.

Humility and modesty bring their own reward. When we restrain our aggressiveness, when we curb our pride, when we subordinate our own demands to the wishes and desires of our fellow man, we open our minds to a better understanding of mankind and thus derive greater joy from life.

The Schulchan Aruch covers a diversified field of conduct for observance by the individual. A few of the rules for personal conduct are:

One should neither be tightfisted nor should he spend his money too freely.

One should not be too jocular and gay, nor morose and melancholy, but should at all times be genial and friendly.

Pride is condemned as a vice and the individual is forbidden from becoming accustomed to it, even in the slightest degree.

Anger is a vice that should be avoided. One should avoid anger to such an extent that he should not become angry even at things that cause anger.

This is the proper path and the path of the righteous— that they who are insulted, do not insult, and that they who hear themselves reviled, answer not.

A man should cultivate the faculty of silence; and even when talking because of the necessity of the situation, he should not talk too much.

A man should not possess unbounded greed for wealth, nor should he be morose and idle; but should be content with that little which is his portion.

One should avoid envy, voluptuousness and passion. This does not mean that one must practice self-denial to the point that he partake not of meat nor wine, nor marry a woman, nor live in a comfortable abode, nor put on respectable clothes. No person shall vow abstinence, nor torment himself with fast days more than is required.

We must not be righteous over much, neither show ourselves overwise.

We should associate ourselves with the righteous and keep away from the wicked who walk in the dark.

We should associate ourselves with the learned.

Each person is required to talk of his neighbor's virtues and to have consideration for his neighbor's property just as he seeks honor for himself and has consideration for his own property. No one may praise himself at his neighbor's expense. He may not do so even if he does not expressly make insulting or uncharitable remarks of his neighbor; he may not compare his own good deeds and wisdom with those of his neighbor in such manner as may cause others to conclude that he is an honorable man, while his neighbor is a despicable person.

One is forbidden to invoke the judgment of heaven against another who has done wrong unto him. He who prays for evil to come on his fellow man, punishment comes to him first.

When we become aware that another is contemplating a crime or embarking on a path of evil, it is our duty to persuade him to improve his conduct, by convincing him that evil deeds are wrong and must not be committed. But this must be done in private (no one else being present), and we must speak quietly and use soft language, and we should convince him that we are urging righteous conduct only for his own good.

We must be careful not to act in any manner which

may tend to create the impression or lead to the suspicion that we have committed some crime.

He who bears a grudge or takes vengeance on his fellow man violates the prohibitory commandment contained in the book of Leviticus, which provides that one shall not take vengeance, nor bear any grudge against the children of his people, and that every person shall love his neighbor as himself.

We must not be a talebearer, even though the thing told be true. Talebearing is a violation of the prohibitory commandment contained in the book of Leviticus, which states that one shall not go up and down as a talebearer among his people.

The commission of slander is also prohibited by this commandment. Even if a person tells the truth—if it is derogatory, he violates this commandment; and if he utters false reports, the guilt is greater. He who receives slanderous reports is worse than the one who gives them. This rule also embraces shades of slander. If, for example, we say that we do not want to tell something about a person because of its nature, and we thereby imply that it is slanderous, this conduct is a violation of the prohibitory commandment contained in the book of Leviticus.

And finally, the Schulchan Aruch recites that there are four classes of persons who are not worthy of communing with God: scorners, hypocrites, liars and slanderers.

In their daily prayers, the Jews pray to God to keep their tongues from evil and their lips from speaking guile. They ask God to open their hearts to His laws, the Torah, and that He permit their souls to pursue His commandments. If Jews desire to have God listen with favor to their prayers, they in turn must keep their tongues from evil and their lips from speaking guile.

The woman's status as to religious and ethical rights and duties is not that of an inferior but of an equal.

Women are required to know the commandments and they are bound by them; and there are imposed upon women the same duties as those imposed upon men in the observance of the religion with this exception: that women are exempt from those positive commandments the observance of which depends upon a definite point of time. To illustrate, women may but are not required to attend synagogue on holidays. This exception is based upon the realization that household duties are so numerous that observance outside of the home may work a severe hardship upon the mother and wife and upon the other members of the household.

During the existence of the Temple, women had access to it in a part separately set aside for their exclusive use. Today, women are admitted to the place of worship on all occasions. In the orthodox synagogue, women and men are separated. This separation takes place so that the worshipper's mind and heart may be completely absorbed in the worship of God and may not be distracted by the presence of or conversation with the other sex.

The woman's place in religion is as important as, and in some respects of even greater importance than that of the man. She is charged with the responsibility of creating and maintaining a religious and devout atmosphere in the home. Children learn of God and of their religion at their mother's knee. One's entire religious life is largely influenced and moulded by the impressions created within him during his childhood when he is closely, constantly and intimately associated with his mother.

There is imposed upon the mother in Israel the duty of imbedding in the mind and heart of the child the religious and ethical principles embraced in Judaism. By her conduct toward her husband, children and the other members of her household, by her observance of the rituals required to be performed in the home, she creates in the child those deep and lasting impressions of justice, righteousness, love of peace, and religion which the child will carry with him throughout life.

It has been stated that she is the crown of her husband and her price is far above rubies.

The code draws no distinction before the law between man and woman. Each is liable without distinction for the commission of wrongful acts and is given the same protection when being judged. Each is given the same right to make atonement religiously for wrongdoing, and expiation is required of each in the same manner. Because she is physically the weaker, greater safeguards are thrown around her. Attention has already been called to the provision of the laws that, where a virgin has been seduced, the male is required to marry the wronged girl and is forever barred from securing a divorce.

Wherever the man appears to be given a greater right or privilege, closer study will disclose that in most instances no preference is in fact intended. This is illustrated in the case of the requirement that not less than ten men shall be present in any assembly for worship (Minyan). The requirement that the ten persons shall be male was not intended as a privilege granted exclusively to men but was fixed rather to free women from this duty, so that their households might not be interfered with.

There is no ban against women deriving education and knowledge on an equality with men. Even in biblical times women were permitted to participate in the study of the Torah and were especially recognized and honored for being learned. One of the prophets of Israel was the prophetess Deborah.

It may thus be said that in Judaism the woman is treated as the equal of the man.

Accordingly, the law in the relationship of man to himself consists largely of the following: He should care for his physical well-being by practicing personal hygiene and cleanliness, by complying with the dietary laws to the extent required by the branch of his faith to which he adheres, by controlling his physical appetites and emotions, by living temperately, by cultivating a pleasant disposition, by avoiding unnecessary physical danger, and by applying the rules of sanitation to his home and to his community—he should care for his mental well-being, by equipping himself with knowledge useful for his daily occupation, whether it be farming or any of the crafts, trades or professions, and with cultural knowledge—and he should equip himself ethically by studying, and making a part of himself, the Scriptures and the religious and ethical code, by learning and practicing self-respect, self-confidence, humility and modesty and by refraining from speaking evil and guile. And thus each person will be enabled to make his full contribution to his own circle, to his community and to society generally.

Chapter XV

SIN

THE word sin is ordinarily used in referring only to those acts which offend God—acts against God rather than against man. In Judaism there is no such distinction. Every act which violates the law is deemed to be against God and is a sin. The failure to pay a workman his wages on the date due, if the employer has the money with which to make such payment, is a violation of God's law and is considered a sin.

As there are six hundred and thirteen commandments in the Torah and, in addition, numberless rules and regulations that have been derived therefrom and included in the Talmud, it is impossible for any person to go through life without committing sin. In fact, it is probably impossible for any person to go through any day of his life without technically violating some one of those commandments, rules or regulations. Having this in mind and realizing this condition, Judaism has subdivided sins into various groups.

Sins are divided into two groups, those committed unwittingly and those committed wittingly. The first group comprises those that are committed inadvertently or accidentally or through lack of knowledge. Those commit-

ted wittingly are acts done deliberately, knowingly or
wilfully.

As to the former group, the Torah provided forgiveness by the performance of some ritual act by the wrongdoer, and, upon compliance with such ritual act, the
wrongdoer was ordinarily absolved.

As to the latter group, those sins which have been committed wittingly, repentance and sincere resolve not to
commit them again were the form of absolution required
of the wrongdoer.

This form of absolution, in either case, had nothing to
do with the requirement that the wrongdoer make restitution to or otherwise satisfy the aggrieved party, and it
had nothing to do with the personal punishment that
might be meted out to the wrongdoer by the civil author-
ities, if the act was of a character for which punishment
was fixed. But to make amends to God, absolution could
be obtained only in the manner above described.

As above stated, sin is forgiven and the sinner is restored to God's favor when he repents and in all sincerity
determines to sin no more. This does not mean that he
can deliberately embark upon the enterprise of sinning,
with the mental reservation that after sinning, he will
repent. Such repentance does not, to God, constitute true
repentance.

Sins are also grouped according to the nature of the
wrongdoing. There are two such divisions. One embraces
acts which do not involve ethical wrongdoing but which
are declared to be sins solely because they violate some
provision of the laws. An example of these would be the
failure to wash one's hands before commencing a meal.

The other division represents acts which in and of themselves are wrong. An illustration of such sins would be committing a murder. These two divisions of wrongdoing are recognized in our present-day statute law. They are expressed by two Latin phrases: "mala prohibita," acts wrongful only because they are forbidden by law, and "mala in se," acts wrongful in and of themselves.

Finally, there is a distinction between an act constituting a violation of an affirmative commandment and an act in violation of a negative commandment. These two groups of sins might be called acts of omission and acts of commission. They are illustrated, the first, by the Fifth Commandment: Thou shalt honor thy father and mother, which is a positive or affirmative commandment, and the second, by the Eighth Commandment: Thou shalt not steal, which is a negative or prohibitory commandment.

Freedom of will has already been discussed under the chapter bearing that heading and reference has also been made to this privilege given to man by God in other parts of the book. It has been made clear that man has been created a free agent and can choose good or evil, in his sole judgment and discretion. He has control over himself to sin or not to sin. The decision lies solely with him. It would appear to be quite easy for man to decide in favor of virtue against vice, in favor of goodness against sinfulness, since man actually has control over that decision and to that extent has control of his destiny. The fact is that it is not so simple. Whatever the reasons may be, and they are unknown to man, sin more often than not is clothed in an attractive form. And we are therefore frequently confronted with the impulse to sin.

It has been stated in the early part of the book that man is born holy, good and free from sin. However, as is so often repeated in the religious writings of Judaism, there is constantly going on within each individual the struggle between the impulse for good (Yetser tov) and the impulse for evil (Yetser hara), each impulse seeking to get the upper hand.

To be victorious over evil, we must strive and strive persistently against it whenever it appears. Maturity is no bulwark against evil. A grown person is just as prone as a child to succumb to temptation. Man must be ever-zealous in maintaining control over his desires if he is to successfully resist evil.

It may be asked why God created sin. The answer to this is not difficult. God wanted man to have freedom of will. It is probably the greatest attribute of our personality. The right of choice, deliberate and conscious, made through the mind, is a quality given to man alone and to no other part of the living world. If he is to have the right of choice, there must be at least two things to choose from, right and wrong, good and evil.

The great scholars and rabbis have been fully conscious of and keenly sensitive to this human impulse to sin, which comes to all of us in our lives. Having full realization of the temptations to which we, human beings, are subject, they have endeavored to formulate warnings and rules which, if followed, will assist the individual to overcome the impulse to sin and keep him free from evil.

We are warned that each sin we commit is but a forerunner of additional sins; that one sin leads to another, and that the smaller sin leads to a greater sin.

We are also warned that once our self-control has been overcome and we have succumbed to temptation, our will to avoid future sin has been correspondingly weakened and we may thereafter become completely helpless in our attempts to resist or avoid sin. Just as good acts help to strengthen our righteousness, so sinful acts weaken our goodness and increase the power of the impulse to sin.

We are further warned that the effects of sin spread beyond our own individual selves. Innocent persons may be completely engulfed in the harm which has come from the wrongdoing of a sinner. Since we are social beings, others will be adversely affected—our family circle, our friends, our business associates and other persons coming in contact with us—and no one can foresee how far and to what extent society may be involved. It is like the injection of poison not only into ourselves but into the very life-stream of society. An illustration of this is the case of a bank employee who through the commission of a series of embezzlements, ultimately causes the bank to fail. Thousands of depositors and their families may be seriously affected.

Even in the case of acts, "mala prohibita," which are not ethically wrong, the misery and destruction wrought may be enormous. The owners of a place of entertainment failed to fireproof some hanging material, thus violating a city ordinance. A fire broke out and spread rapidly because of these non-fireproofed decorations. Many persons were burned or trampled to death, bringing bereavement to many families, wives, children and other dependents. Illustrations can be added without number, where a wrongdoing of an apparently minor nature has resulted in great misfortune. There are instances given in the Scriptures of disaster brought about by the sin of a single individual.

Another warning of the rabbis is that when we set a bad example, others are induced to become sinners. This is well illustrated in the associations of children or adolescents. One youth acts wrongfully and speaks or even boasts of it to the others of the group. The thoughts instilled in the minds of the other members, especially where the sin is garbed attractively, may result in others emulating the wrongdoer. This is equally true with grown-ups. Excessive drinking, gambling for large stakes and even seriously offensive habits have been introduced to persons of mature years by acquaintances and friends with whom they have associated.

The scholars and rabbis advise that one should not tempt temptation—that headstrong is the man who invites temptation in order to display his self-control. When temptation comes on the scene, they teach that it is wisdom to run away. Temptation should be avoided, not sought. He is wise who consistently follows this principle.

The scholars and rabbis further advise that one should pray daily as a means of resisting the impulse for evil. By prayer, the individual constantly keeps alive in his mind the utter folly of evil-doing and its baneful results, and in that way he is reinforced in his determination to be good and not evil.

Idleness is an encourager of evil. We are safest when we keep our minds occupied. There is no opportunity for evil to seep in. If part of this mental occupation is with one's religion and with God by means of prayer, then we certainly shall help ourselves in the avoidance of doing evil.

When we love God, when we pray to Him, with all our heart, with all our soul, the evil impulse is held down and our natural good impulse holds sway.

God is a forgiving God. He understands that He has made man frail, subject to human temptation, that perfection is only Himself, and that each of us will sin. Therefore, when we pray to Him and purify our hearts and our souls and determine not to sin again, and if we live up to this determination, then we are forgiven by God for our sins.

Chapter XVI

RETRIBUTION

LIKE all other religions, Judaism cannot give definite and specific answers to all the questions that arise in our finite minds concerning life, death and the destiny of man.

In the chapters on FREEDOM OF WILL, on PRAYER and on IMMORTALITY, reward for good acts and punishment for evil deeds are indirectly touched upon. We have noted under FREEDOM OF WILL that the righteous sometimes meet with distress and harm through no fault of their individual selves but because of something done or omitted by another member of society. In PRAYER, we shall see the disappointment of the individual, because God apparently has failed to listen to his prayer, to the granting of which he believed himself entitled. In IMMORTALITY, we shall find that many have a deep-seated hope in a personal immortality, in a life eternal, with the retention of entity in some form, based on the belief that the universe is founded on justice, that the principle of justice would be violated if there were not recompense in some other world to the person who, although acting righteously, has met only with grief and tragedy.

As has been stated at the very beginning of the book, there is nothing in the Torah that recognizes any sort of heaven or hell, or makes any provision for reward or pun-

ishment after death. Thus, the only answer, as to reward
and punishment in the hereafter, must be faith in God;
that God, who is a God of Justice, will in some manner
square accounts; that His ways are inscrutable; that we
must be satisfied with the faith that somewhere on the
long road through eternity we shall each eventually receive our just deserts.

When we attempt to probe God's motives or intentions with respect to some of the happenings in this life,
we cannot find an answer or even any plausible or reasonable explanation. We come up against a blank wall. We
must then fall back on our faith, that whatever God has
willed, He has willed for a purpose, which to Him is sufficient to justify the act. These are the mysteries which it
has not been given to man to understand. We must accept
them as God's will.

In the early part of the book it has been stated that faith
is reached largely through reason but that there is a limit
to intelligence and knowledge beyond which the human
mind cannot go; that when that point is reached, faith is
based upon an inner urge and desire to believe rather
than upon reason. Retribution (that is: reward for good
acts and punishment for evil deeds), in so far as it may
come beyond this life, falls within this latter category.
Thus belief in such retribution is based upon an inner
urge and desire to believe.

Since Judaism teaches primarily a way of life and tells
its adherents not to be concerned with the hereafter, and
that the hereafter will take care of itself, there is no definite principle in Judaism relating to reward or punishment. Hence in Judaism retribution after life is more in

the nature of a hope or fear rather than a definite principle of faith.

Some rabbis and scholars, however, have upheld retribution as one of the tenets of Judaism. This has been based largely upon the wording of the Second Commandment, that portion which reads: Thou shalt not bow down unto them nor serve them; for I the Lord thy God am a jealous God, visiting the iniquity of the fathers upon the children unto the third and fourth generation of them that hate Me; and showing mercy unto the thousandth generation of them that love Me and keep My commandments.

They believe that the reference to the visiting of the iniquity of the fathers upon the children and the showing of loving kindness to the thousandth generation, is not limited by the earlier portion of this commandment —that we shall have no other gods and that we shall not worship idols—but that it applies to punishment for evil deeds and reward for righteous acts.

Maimonides, who enunciated the principles of faith referred to in the chapter on the NATURE OF GOD, was a firm believer in retribution. His eleventh principle states that he firmly believes that God rewards those who keep His commandments and punishes those who transgress them.

The Prophets were much troubled by the vagueness of the Torah with regard to retribution. They all stressed the point that God was a God of justice, and in their teachings they emphasized the hope that in the hereafter there would be reward for the righteous and punishment for the wrongdoer.

And in the Talmud there are included interpretations of passages in the Torah that would seem to hold forth the promise of reward in the hereafter for obedience to God's commandments in this life. There are even imaginative descriptions of paradise and hell. All these, however, are merely the yearnings of humanity for the hope of a hereafter—that this life cannot be the end, but only the beginning of things to come.

There is also expressed in the Talmud the viewpoint that there is not necessarily any reward in the hereafter for goodness, but that there is punishment for evil.

This viewpoint is based upon the following reasoning: The Scriptures often refer to God as a just God. God has given man freedom of will. Man has the ability to choose and decide between good and evil. If he chooses good, he is doing what God expects him to do; and since it is God's wish for man to select good, he must be good for goodness' own sake and not because of the hope or expectation of any special credit or reward. If, however, man chooses evil, he has exercised his will deliberately and voluntarily in favor of wrongdoing. Thus, since God is just, He will do justice by punishing the person who has chosen wrongdoing. The argument concludes that the ability to choose must carry with it punishment for selecting evil. If this were not so, nothing could be placed on the scales held by the individual, in favor of good as against evil. If there were no punishment or other detriment involved, why should not a person choose evil, especially if he finds evil attractive?

Accordingly, retribution in the hereafter for evil doing,

although not a definite principle of faith, has been considered by many as part of Judaism.

If we examine the subject a little more closely, we find that, by and large, retribution comes to one during his lifetime, that the very act of wrongdoing brings in its train, punishment, often meted out in some form before death.

We are all too prone to judge happiness and unhappiness from external appearances. We see a man who is unscrupulous in his business dealings; he has thereby amassed large sums of money; he does not seem to be bothered or in any way affected by his wrongful conduct; he has all the luxuries of life; he lives in a grand state; and it would seem as if he were even being rewarded, not punished, for his evil doing.

Upon further study, we may find that this man may not be enjoying real contentment and real happiness. His family life, his association with his wife, with his children, with his other kin, the relationship between him and those whom he considers his friends, may not be of a character that leads to inner contentment, peace of mind and happiness. The arrogance that he may have developed in pursuing his evil ways may not only have soured his life but may also have adversely affected his relationship with his family and others. As a result, he may not derive from that relationship those things which the gentle, the humble and the kindly derive from their associations.

We must analyze and understand the true meaning of contentment and happiness, before we arrive at the conclusion that some particular person is contented and happy.

We all strive for different things, each one seeking to satisfy certain desires and ambitions. But no matter what one's desires or ambitions may be, no matter what his station in life or his business or professional association or employment, happiness means basically the following: an inner feeling of contentment and peace with one's self and with one's external world; a love for one's family and other kin; an affection for one's friends, and a benign and kindly feeling toward society generally—and the knowledge that one's family and other kin and friends reciprocate such love and affection; and that society, to the extent that he touches it, has regard and liking for him.

In addition, there is the freedom from monetary worry. We should have sufficient earnings to provide for the daily requirements of food, clothing, shelter and education for ourselves and our families. There should be a surplus to enable us to partake of the ordinary relaxations and pleasures of life. And, finally, we should have sufficient savings to give us a sense of security in the event of illness and for old age.

These latter items are important, but the fundamental basis of happiness is inner contentment, and that love and affection which are given and reciprocated.

If we could apply these tests to the situations where apparently evil has triumphed and righteousness has failed, we would find that, in most instances, true contentment and happiness have not been attained by the wicked or the evil-doer.

In a further study of ourselves and of our associates, we shall find that as one lie leads to another, so one truth leads to another. We, in reality, reward ourselves by being good, and we punish ourselves by being bad. Virtue (goodness) brings its own reward just as vice (evil) brings its own punishment. This thought is illustrated by the daily occurrences in our law courts. A witness who deliberately lies, finds himself, upon cross-examination, adding lie to lie in order to justify and conceal his previous lie, until the entire house of cards falls down upon him to his utter confusion; whereas the witness who will not be drawn from the truth, will find in the end that his testimony will be accepted and his cross-examiner discredited.

No one should ever forget that all life is part of a grand blueprint; that life and the universe are organized—intelligently, meaningfully and purposefully. One cannot fail God's laws without having such violations catch up with him, ultimately and in his very lifetime, unless his life should be terminated so quickly as to prevent it. If he lives long enough, his reward and punishment will be meted out to him, in some form, during his lifetime. As honesty is the best policy, so to be righteous and to live one's life in God's way and as He wills it, will bring its rewards.

No one can reach and pass through his mature life without realizing that retribution is a living, vital force in this world; that few escape it for better or for worse. It may be that some of us believe that we have not been rewarded for our good deeds, but surely very few persons who have committed wrongdoing, do not, sooner or later, realize that they are being punished, that retribution is being visited upon them for their wrongful acts.

Our conscience often plays strange tricks on us. Although, by arguing the thing through with ourselves, we sometimes come to believe that we were justified in having done some wrong, sooner or later we shall find the still, small voice of conscience reproaching us, and the symbolic finger of scorn pointing at us for the wrong we have committed.

No person, whatever his station in life, economic or social, has any monopoly on goodness or wickedness. All poor men are not good and all rich men are not bad. Indeed, there are many poor persons who have vices and serious ones, and there are many human beings, rich in material things, who have many good traits.

Each person should judge himself and be judged by his own personality and heart. And he may be sure that there will be retribution for him in this world, based upon his just deserts.

Chapter XVII

MESSIAH

THERE is no reference to a Messiah in the Torah. Variations of the Hebrew word "mashiah" (anointed) are used, but simply to describe the priest as anointed. The thought of a Messiah which runs through the other books of the Scriptures, contemplates the birth of a human being who will become an ideal king. He will rule with wisdom and justice, eliminate war and conquest, destroy all the instruments of war and establish peace among the people.

The golden age of the Jews as a nation was ushered in with the reign of King David, who became ruler in the eleventh century before the present era. This period continued through the reigns of David and Solomon. After Solomon's death, internal dissension increased. In addition, the pressure against the Jewish kingdom from powerful neighboring kingdoms became greater and greater.

The first great misfortune, that occurred to the Jewish nation, was the split into two parts—Israel, representing the ten northern tribes, and Judah, embracing the two tribes located in the southern part of the kingdom. The northern portion was then overrun by the Assyrians and the ten tribes were carried off into captivity. These ten tribes of Israel disappeared and no trace of them has ever been found. The difficulties of the southern part, Judah, comprising the two remaining tribes, steadily increased, and culminated in the sacking of their kingdom and the carrying off of the population into captivity in Babylon. This occurred in the sixth century before the present era.

Thus, with the ending of the golden age and the accumulations of the troubles of the Jewish nation, both externally and internally, it was natural for the people to look to God for the coming of some human being who would have the personality, the ability and genius to reunite the Jews, defeat their enemies, bring peace and tranquility to the land and renew the days of old, of David and Solomon. In this manner there came into being the idea of a Messiah.

He would be a man who would love God, truly believe in Him and completely comply with His laws. He would be a man who would gather the Jews together again in their own land, who would become their king, who would bring the people back to the love of God and to obedience to and compliance with His laws. The Messianic times, a new golden age, a period of complete happiness, would then be ushered in and the Jews would then be so perfect in the knowledge and worship of God that all nations would seek enlightenment in the house of the God of Jacob, and all mankind would then live by and in the spirit of the laws of God.

The prophets, Isaiah and Micah, both spoke of this future Messianic period. Isaiah said: And it shall come to pass that the mountain of the Lord's house shall be established in the top of the mountains, and shall be exalted above the hills; and all nations and many peoples shall go up to the mountain of the Lord, to the house of the God of Jacob; and the Lord will teach us of His ways, and we will walk in his paths; for out of Zion shall go forth the law, and the word of the Lord from Jerusalem. It is in these sayings that Isaiah made the immortal statement: And He shall judge between the nations, and shall decide for many peoples; and they shall beat their swords into plowshares, and their spears into pruning-hooks; nation shall not lift up sword against nation, neither shall they learn war anymore. It would be a time when: The wolf shall dwell with the lamb, and the leopard shall lie down with the kid; and the calf and the young lion and the fatling together.

In this Messiah there would rest the spirit of the Lord, the spirit of wisdom and understanding, the spirit of counsel and might, the spirit of knowledge and the fear of the Lord. He would not judge after the sight of his eyes, nor decide after the hearing of his ears; but with righteousness would he judge the poor and decide with equity for the meek of the land. Righteousness would be the girdle of his loins, and faithfulness the girdle of his reins. He would be a human being who would love and obey God and who would be the beloved of God.

Nowhere in the Scriptures is there any thought or suggestion of a divine or supernatural Messiah who by reason of or through his divine powers would create an ideal world out of our most imperfect one. The idea of a supernatural Messiah, chosen by God to bring about universal truth, justice and happiness, was developed and took great hold on the Jews some time after the fall of the Maccabees, about the time Herod became King of the Jews.

Herod lived shortly prior to the commencement of the present era. The country was under Roman control and Herod was king by grace of the Romans and subject to their will. Rule by Herod, under Roman control, was extremely harsh. Herod was constantly at war. The peasantry was brutalized by this warfare. Large numbers of the male population had been either maimed or killed. War was the scourge of the people. Great sorrow, misery and distress were widespread through the land. Large portions of the population were neglected, degraded and even abandoned. The people yearned for deliverance from their oppressors.

At or about this time, there were three definite religious sects among the Jews. There were the Sadducees comprised largely of the wealthy class. They were the patricians and aristocrats often connected by marriage with the high priests and the presiding officers of the Temple. They sought worldly success. They included in their ranks the Jews who were powerful politically, who had the ear of the Roman governor. The second group was the Pharisees, embracing laymen, scholars and artisans, who, though generally well situated economically, were not interested in politics, but were devoted rather to their religion. The third class was the Essenes. They lived in a sort of communal life. All their worldly goods were apparently administered by a selected committee for the benefit of the group. They were extremely devout and led a most holy life.

The Sadducees did not believe in a Messiah. The Pharisees believed in a Messiah of a national character, one who would be mortal, a human being who would come to lead the Jews to throw off the yoke of Roman oppression and bring peace and contentment to the Jews, as a nation. The Essenes were devout believers in a supernatural Messiah. They expected the arrival momentarily of a Messiah who would bring to the people individually, enduring happiness.

It was natural that the common people generally, suffering sorrow, misery and distress, should eagerly respond and turn to the belief of the Essenes in a divine Messiah, and they awaited his arrival with burning desire.

Jesus either was an Essene or was sympathetic to and followed their principles, and the Christians have embraced the concept that Jesus was the Messiah. The Jews deny this concept. They say that, according to the Scriptures, the Messiah will usher in the Messianic period. This period has been described in the earlier part of this chapter. It will be a period of universal peace, justice and righteousness. Admittedly, such a period has not yet come; there has been neither world peace, justice nor righteousness.

The orthodox belief is that in God's good time a Messiah will come, the kind of a Messiah and the sort of a Messianic period, described by Isaiah and Micah.

The conservative branch of Judaism embodies in its prayer book the same views as those of the orthodox, but many of its adherents reinterpret this concept.

The reform synagogue does not regard the coming of a Messiah as part of its religious concepts and does not consider the thought of a Messiah an essential part of Judaism. The reform synagogue treats symbolically the concept of the coming of a Messianic period. It teaches rather the belief in the ultimate establishment on earth of the kingdom of God, of universal brotherhood, justice, truth and peace, which it describes as its Messianic goal, and for which all Jews must strive.

This latter viewpoint may be deemed to be the modern interpretation. When the whole world has been won to the belief and faith in the one, living and loving God, and to the acceptance and practice of His laws, when all the peoples of the earth have reached the state of the true brotherhood of man—then there will be realized the Messianic period, envisioned by the Scriptures.

Chapter XVIII

RESURRECTION

THE belief in Judaism as to resurrection, and the nature of such belief have been constantly changing. Among the early Hebrews there was no belief in resurrection. Shortly after Daniel, who lived around the fifth or sixth century before the present era, there appears to have been a definite belief that there would be resurrection for the righteous.

Along with the development of the thought of a Messiah who would lead the Jews back to Palestine and there recreate the Jewish nation in an ideal kingdom under ideal conditions, there arose the belief in resurrection. The Jews visioned a reconstituted world where all the discord of life would vanish and all disappointment disappear, and where the good and the faithful who had suffered so much, would rise from their graves and come back to a life of peace and happiness.

Their faith was deep and their hope fervent. They did not seek to explain how this phenomenon of resurrection would occur, nor did they endeavor to picture the details of the new world. It was sufficient for them that it had been promised.

As was shown under MESSIAH, at or about the time of the commencement of the present era, there were three Jewish sects, the Sadducees, the Pharisees and the Essenes, the Sadducees rejecting the belief in a Messiah, the Pharises and the Essenes maintaining such belief. Accompanying the belief in a Messiah, there was the belief in resurrection.

The Pharisees and the Essenes deeply believed in a physical resurrection and the common people, who were the forgotten men of that time, embraced this belief. Many who had been bereaved held the belief that with the coming of the Messiah, there would also occur the resurrection of their beloved dead, and that reunion between the deceased and the living would then take place.

The concept of resurrection varied over the years. There were those who believed that resurrection would consist of the physical resurrection of the body. They believed that although upon death the body and the soul were separated, resurrection would bring them together again, that such reunion would occur with the coming of the Messiah, and that this condition would exist during the entire Messianic period. There were those who believed that resurrection would come only to the spirit, that the spirit would be resurrected and clothed in a body of glory and light.

There also existed at one time a controversy as to whether resurrection was the privilege of the Jews alone, or whether it applied to all humanity, regardless of their beliefs. There was also a difference of opinion whether resurrection would come only to those who were righteous, or to the righteous and unrighteous alike.

Those Jews who devoutly believe in resurrection rely upon the belief that God is a God of justice. They say that since God selected the Jews as His instrumentality for bringing to the world the concept of His unity and His laws for the guidance of humanity, He will reward them for the pain, agony, torture and the untimely deaths suffered by them over the ages.

They believe that it is consistent with their thoughts of God that those who have been devout and have suffered persecution and even martyrdom because of their insistence in keeping the faith and enunciating it to the world, should be rewarded, or at least made whole. From this reasoning, they induce the concept that there will be a physical resurrection, a resurrection of the body with the reincorporation of the soul, and that thereafter there will be a long period of life on earth during which they will be rewarded or made whole, for their devotion and suffering.

During the middle ages this belief was especially prevalent. One country after another took a hand at persecution. There was probably not a single country in which the Jews dwelt during this period, that did not torture and kill Jews because of their religion. It was largely their passionate belief in resurrection that sustained the Jews during their afflictions, tribulations and martyrdom. Nothing could make them deny their faith, their belief in the one God who would in His own time bring them back into this world.

The thought that there will be a physical resurrection and that physical resurrection will take place in Palestine when the Messiah comes, has persisted strongly to the present day, and there are many Jews today who have faith in this belief. There have been Jews who, upon reaching old age, have journeyed from all parts of the world, including this country, to Israel. Their purpose has been to spend their remaining days in that country and to be buried there, in the holy land, in order that, when the Messiah arrives, they will rise from the dead and live again in Israel.

The modern trend in Judaism is definitely away from the belief in resurrection, particularly physical resurrection. The thought of resurrection has been merged in the reform synagogue and largely in the conservative synagogue, with the belief in the immortality of the soul. Immortality of the soul rather than resurrection can now be considered an integral tenet of Judaism.

It has been said that Godfaithfulness seems to point, not to the fulfillment of the promise of resurrection, but rather to the realization of those higher expectations of personal immortality, which are sown in every human soul and are part of its very nature.

Chapter XIX

IMMORTALITY

SINCE Judaism as a religion is primarily a way of life, one seeks in vain in the Torah for any definite exposition of Judaism's viewpoint as to immortality. It is implied in the Torah rather than expressed therein.

Immortality, in its broad sense, is the conception of some continuity of existence after death and the dissolution of the body.

It has been said that man is arrogant in assuming that he is immortal, that he is beyond the laws visible throughout nature, of birth, growth, decline and complete end upon death. It has been said that, in comparison with the vastness and extent of the universe, man is so insignificant in size and his home in the universe is so small in space that it is presumptuous for man to consider his destiny different from that of any other part of nature.

The answer to this view is, that of the entire universe and of all creation, man alone is Godly, man alone has a soul, a part of the infinite within him. He alone has the ability to contemplate and to be in contact with God, and the ability to distinguish between right and wrong, good and evil. These powers, given to man and to man alone, must have been given purposefully. They would seem to have been given to man by God in vain, if all were to cease and end completely with death. Man has the right to believe that he is separate and apart from other forms of life, that since he has been selected as their master, he is worthy of an end different from that of the rest of nature.

Judaism recognizes the existence of the soul and considers the soul a part of God. Since God is eternal, it must follow that the soul is eternal. Thus, there is also the recognition in Judaism of immortality.

The question arises whether there is, in immortality, the element of entity, the continuity of recognition of one's own self after death; whether our ego, our feeling of separateness from other beings, our consciousness of individuality, our personality, continue after death— whether there is a personal immortality.

We know that in the animal world, there is some instinctive or automatic sense of entity, the sense of self-preservation being probably as highly developed in animals as it is in human beings. The instinct of self-preservation is essentially the attempt to prevent destruction of self and to maintain one's entity. It can be argued, therefore, that, since an animal, even though it has no soul, has a sense of entity and of individualism, and possibly in the same manner and to the same extent as a human being, this sense of entity comes from having life, rather than from having a soul. Repeating the thought in another form, since animals have no souls, the feeling of entity must come from their feeling of being alive, that is, from life.

Applying this conclusion to human beings, our feeling of entity must come from our being alive and not from our having a soul. Hence, the soul may have no relationship to entity. If the foregoing is accepted as correct, it may be urged that upon the termination of life, entity ceases and the survival or continuity of the soul after death does not carry with it the retention of the ego.

The concept of immortality, accordingly, is not necessarily that of a personal immortality, of a retention of entity after death, but rather the return to God of the soul resident in each of us. Thus, immortality, in a broad sense, means the joinder with and absorption into God of our soul after death. The soul which is immortal comes to us from God upon birth and goes back to God upon death. The dust shall return to the earth as it was, and the spirit shall return to God who gave it. This continued contact with and reabsorption into God may be considered immortality.

Notwithstanding these conclusions, there is in all of us a deep-seated hope of a personal immortality that, upon death, there shall not be an end of our entity, but that such entity shall thereafter continue in some form. Such basic desire, hope and aspiration, for a personal immortality, are in themselves some indication of God's intention of giving us this continuity of self. Our belief in God is largely based upon a similar, deep emotion and desire to believe in Him, and if that is so with our belief in God, it may also be so with respect to personal immortality. We have this yearning for an indefinable hereafter. There is a longing for something after life.

It would appear to be inconsistent with the basic principle of justice to cut off with death the continuity of such phases of life as love. Upon the death of a child, the love of the parent remains alive and deep. The parent's entire being protests against any permanent severance upon death. There is deep within him the belief, almost assurance, that upon his death there will be some form of reunion between his soul and that of his dead child, that there will be an individual, realized continuity of such love.

The hope for a personal immortality is largely based upon the concept that God is justice. When we consider the uncertainty of life and the misery and wretchedness which have been and are the lot of so many people, where happiness and misfortune are not equitably distributed, where the good are often the sufferers and the wicked appear to be the beneficiaries, there is the feeling that there must be some point at which these wrongs are righted. If these wrongs are not righted for the individual in this world, the hope is that somewhere in the hereafter there will be an evening-up and that justice will be done.

It is not important for the human being to conceive of the kind of an existence of which the soul will be a part, when he reaches the state of immortality. Any attempt to describe the condition of immortality must be regarded merely as a matter of imagination rather than of knowledge. We humans do not know how it is ordered nor can we imagine its operation. A complete explanation of the future beyond this world has not been and will probably never be vouchsafed us. Perhaps this was deliberately intended by God, for if we knew, it might have some adverse effect upon our freedom of will and our activity in this world.

The human being is willing to take a chance on personal immortality. The thought of chance involves the element of hope. The existence of chance makes a great difference, the difference between resignation and hope. Thus, in Judaism, the concept of the continuity of entity after death exists as a hope, rather than as a principle of faith.

For those in Judaism who desire to go beyond merely the hope of the continuity of entity and who wish to believe that in immortality there is the retention of entity after death, immortality in that sense may be deemed to be realized by the propagation of the race. The parent continues his entity and personality in his child. In the child there is the continuity of the personality and entity of the parent. This continuity of entity and personality from generation to generation may be deemed to constitute immortality.

There is another form of continuity which may be deemed to be immortal, and that is the continued remembrance of the human being by his own and by succeeding generations. Man has the power to make a contribution to his fellow man. Where this contribution results in benefit to society, that man's personality can be said to live on indefinitely. Any contribution a person makes is, in a sense, the giving of a part of himself. Where that contribution results in good, the human being has made a permanent impress of his personality on society.

Our good deeds, our good acts, no matter how small or large, have a permanent effect, the scope and extent of which we may not and cannot visualize or realize. It is like the throwing of a stone into a pool of water, from the impact of which ripples reach out in every direction. To the extent that we bend society and life to our will by means of these good acts and deeds, we achieve a sort of impersonal immortality.

It has been written that we have not the elements for a solution to the question as to whether there is immortality. Whatever visions beyond there may be, what larger hopes and what ultimate harmonies, if such there are in store, will come in God's good time. It is not for us to anticipate them or lift the veil where God has left it down.

Chapter XX

THE MISSION

EVERY organized religion embraces among its beliefs that of an earthly mission. Each believes that the adoption and observance of its religion or the acceptance and performance of its principles will be of great value to humanity. This is true of the three great western religions—Mohammedanism, Christianity and Judaism. Each seeks to attain its goal in a different manner.

Mohammedanism believes that force is a proper and justifiable method, if need be, to bring about conversion to its faith. From the time of its foundation by Mohammed, compulsion was resorted to and many who refused to be converted were put to the sword.

Since the creation of the church, Christianity has brought the pagan world into its fold by proselyting, and today many branches of the Christian Church are most active in their missionary work in every quarter of the globe.

Although there have been times in the history of the Jews when they have actively proselyted, Judaism is not a proselyting religion. It accepts but does not seek converts. What Judaism strives to accomplish is the acceptance of the belief in monotheism and the adoption and practice by all peoples of the ethical principles revealed to the Jews by God at Mount Sinai through Moses. It seeks to establish the belief in the one living and loving God and the adoption and practice of His way of life. This way of life is one based upon justice, righteousness and peace and upon the commandment laid down in the book of Leviticus that we shall love our neighbors as ourselves.

Thus, in the same manner that the other modern great religions embrace missions as part of their earthly goals, so Judaism embraces, as one of its tenets, the belief in an earthly mission.

The Jews believe that they are qualified to carry on this mission. Many peoples have had special abilities, talents and even genius in connection with certain phases of life. The two well-known illustrations of this special genius are the Greeks and the Romans, the former—for beauty and art, and the latter—for law and organization. From the time of Abraham, through the biblical and post-biblical periods and down to the present day, the Jews, as a people, have had a genius for religion and ethics. They have been, through the ages, and they are today, the people of the Book.

The Jews have been called the chosen people of God. This expression has been misinterpreted and misunderstood by many. God did not choose the Jews because He wished them to be His favorite children or because He wished to bestow favors upon them. God has chosen and sanctified them as His special representatives to perform a task, a mission.

Their task, their mission, is to bring to and help to establish throughout the world—the belief in the oneness and unity of God, and the knowledge of and compliance with His laws. Jews must spread and help to bring about this belief, knowledge and compliance, not by compulsion or violence, but by precept and example. As God's servants and messengers, they must become and remain a light unto the nations of the world. By living noble and holy lives, by compliance with His laws, they are to set an example, and thus influence all peoples to become noble and holy, and to conduct their lives in compliance with God's laws. Jews must be holy as He is holy. It is their duty to participate in winning the whole world to God, so that all people will serve God, believe in Him and follow His laws.

God selected Abraham to be the founder of the nation which would have this mission to perform. He directed Abraham to leave his country, his father's house, his kinsfolk, in order to spread the knowledge of God's unity.

This trust, imposed upon the Jews, was confirmed by God, by revelation through Moses, at Mount Sinai: Thus shalt thou say to the house of Jacob and tell the children of Israel: Now, therefore, if ye hearken unto My voice, indeed, and keep My covenant, then ye shall be Mine own treasure from among all peoples; and ye shall be unto Me a kingdom of priests and a holy nation.

In the book of Isaiah, reference is made to this trusteeship of the Jews: I the Lord have called thee in righteousness, and have taken hold of thy hand, and kept thee, and set thee for a covenant of the people, for a light of the nations; to open the blind eyes, to bring out the prisoners from the dungeon, and them that sit in darkness out of the prison-house.

The Jews consecrated their lives to this purpose.

There was backsliding by the Jews, from time to time, both as a nation and as individuals, for which they suffered severely. There were, however, many Jews, at all times, even during these periods of lapses, who were true to their consecration and who kept brightly burning the light and the glory of their trust, continuously from generation to generation, down to the present day.

In spite of the destruction of their nation and their dispersion, the Jews have survived, and have thrived and remained a people as young and as vibrant in spirit as they were during the golden age of David. The reason that may be ascribed for their survival is that the Jews have not completed their mission, they have not reached the goal set for them by God.

Since their dispersion, the great majority of the Jews have strictly adhered to the laws as revealed by God for their guidance and living. They have always been keenly and deeply aware of their consecration to God and the necessity for obedience to His laws. In a world of much vice and sin, they have exercised self-restraint and self-control, and have maintained a high standard of ethics, resulting in a healthy body and mind. God required of them holiness and they strove for it, throughout the centuries, with all their hearts and souls.

The Jews have practiced separateness throughout their history. They have remained a people separate and distinct from other peoples. The principle of separateness was constantly followed. This principle was adopted and rigidly adhered to, not because the Jews thought they were better than other peoples, but because they recognized the fact that if they were to fulfill their trust, they could not permit themselves to be absorbed.

It is not intended by separateness that the Jews shall keep aloof. There is nothing in their religion nor in their laws that restricts social, economic and political relationship to or association with their neighbors and other members of society. On the contrary, such association and mingling are necessary, if by their example they are to influence the way of life of others. When God created the Jews a people of priests, He did not intend that as a priestly class they would be removed and withdrawn from society, devoted solely to contemplation and prayer. He intended them to be priests who would participate in every phase of life as an integral part of society, and thus bring to the world knowledge of Him and of His laws. Israel became not alone the servant of God but the servant of humanity as well.

By separateness, it is intended that they shall retain their customs and practices, and that they shall not intermarry. Non-intermarriage is of the essence. Intermarriage would result in a merger of the Jewish people with others and the loss of their distinct identity. If they are to be true to their trust, and to continue to work for its fulfillment, it is essential that they continue to maintain this separateness.

Because they are trustees for God, their responsibilities have been and are greater and heavier than those of others. They have always had the courage of their convic-

tions. They have never flinched in their duties and the*j*
have risked and sacrificed greatly, even with their lives, to
carry out their trusteeship.

As long as they adhere to their trust, as long as they
earnestly, sincerely and steadfastly pursue their endeavor
to fulfill it—so long shall they overcome their persecu-
tors and oppressors, and they shall survive and continue
to be the eternal people—old in years, but always youth-
ful and strong in spirit.

Their task has been partly accomplished. They have
given to the world the Scriptures, the basis of religion.
The Scriptures contain the Ten Commandments, which
are the foundation of ethics. Thus the cornerstones of
our present-day civilization and society—religion and
ethics—have been contributed by the Jews. Idolatry has
been largely eliminated in the civilized countries of the
world. Judaism is the mother of the two new great religions, Christianity and Mohammedanism. These are
outgrowths of Judaism and are largely founded upon it.
Both have combatted idolatry, adopted monotheism and
have preached a way of life based upon the ethics taught
by Judaism.

The mission of the Jews has not, however, been completed. War, the terrible scourge of mankind through all
recorded history, has not been eliminated. Justice, righteousness and peace, the fundamentals of God's laws, do
not reign supreme. Until they do, the Jews cannot consider their mission as having been fulfilled, and they must
carry on.

The Jews must not become disheartened nor must they
give up, because some of their own stray away or be-

cause they are prevented by others from carrying on. To resign themselves to failure or to deliberately give up and thus to break the covenant with God, made by Abraham and Moses on their behalf, is sinful. God has only contempt for the faint-hearted and the cowardly, but God respects, admires and loves the courageous.

We humans cannot always be in the position of beseeching God for favors. We must sometimes work for God without counting the consequences. The Jews have had through the ages a deathless urge to fulfill their trust and they never stopped to consider the cost. Each generation must carry on, until the job has been done, done well and fully completed.

The Jews are not agreed among themselves as to how their mission shall be accomplished. Since the elimination of the ghetto, the throwing off of its shackles, and the entry of the Jew into the full life of the nation in which he resides, the hope and belief in a Messiah and in the coming of the Messianic times have to many lost their attraction.

Among many of the Jews, there has developed the view that they can carry on their trust in the land of their birth and upbringing, rather than as part of a Jewish nation which is to rise again in Palestine. This has been particularly true with many who have joined and become part of the reform movement.

To them, they will be fulfilling their trust if, by their personal individual conduct, they have set an example of righteousness for the peoples among whom they live, thus contributing their influence in bringing about ideal governments based on justice, righteousness and peace, as contemplated by the Scriptures for the Messianic period; and the Scriptures have been interpreted by them accordingly. Some, indeed, regard the dispersion of the Jews as a divine act, intended to scatter them among all nations, so that their mission can be accomplished more quickly and effectively.

However, many Jews, possibly a majority of them, have felt that their mission can be accomplished only if the Jews again create a nation in their homeland, Palestine. Then, not alone as individuals scattered and living among the different countries of the world, but also as a free nation, with complete sovereignty, will they be able to put into practical effect the principles of God's laws. It is their view that the finest elements of the human soul can flourish best in the fertile soil of a nation. Israel, the nation, as God's servant, will become a light unto all nations.

In other words, Jews will help to bring about an ideal world by the creation of a nation in Israel, which will serve as a model for other nations, while many other Jews will continue to remain scattered throughout the world and, by their holy and exemplary conduct, will set an example for those among whom they dwell.

In any event, if Jews are to be true to their trust, they must comply and live in accordance with the spirit of God's laws. As they have a covenant with and are consecrated to God, the private and public life of each and every Jew must be holy. Not by might, nor by power, but through the spirit—by precept and example—they must carry out their trusteeship and show the world how people must live if there is to be universal justice, righteousness and peace.

Then the improvement of all peoples must and will come in God's own time, and the goal, to bring about the kingdom of God, here on earth, and into the hearts of all of God's children, will be attained—and then and only then will the world be blessed with enduring peace and with the true brotherhood of man.

In that day shall the Lord be King over all the earth; in that day shall the Lord be One and His name One.

Chapter XXI

JEWS AND CHRISTIANS—RELATIONSHIP

A LARGE proportion of the human population is of the Christian faith. Our present-day society and civilization are dominated and influenced by Christianity. Most of the Jews scattered throughout the world dwell in countries, the majority of whose people embrace the Christian religion. Christians are the neighbors of the Jews. Many Christians and Jews bear the relationship to each other of employer and employee, and of employee and employer. Christians and Jews are intimately associated together in business, the arts, the sciences and the professions. There is constant and continuous social mingling between them.

Accordingly, no study or discussion of Judaism, of what it means and stands for today, no modern interpretation of Judaism, can ignore Christianity in its present relationship with Judaism.

Although the fundamental theological principles and beliefs of Judaism and Christianity, as organized religions, vary in aims and practices, they are similar in a number of respects. Both believe—that each human being has within him a soul, a part of the Divinity—that each of us has been given by God freedom of will, the ability to choose between good and evil—that God is interested in each individual—that God·can be reached through prayer—and that revelation was made by God to the human race through the patriarchs, Moses and the other prophets.

The code of ethics of Christianity is derived from Judaism's code and the variations between them, if any, are minor. The crux of both is embodied in the golden rule. This rule is expressed by the Christians: All things therefore whatsoever ye would that men should do unto you, even so do ye also unto them. While the Jews express it in the maxim: And what is displeasing to thyself, that do not unto any other; and in another form: Not to do unto one's fellow what is hateful to oneself.

This rule is a corollary of and derived from the commandment embodied in both religions, contained in the book of Leviticus: Thou shalt love thy neighbor as thyself. The ultimate ethical goal of both is the attainment on earth of universal justice, righteousness and peace and the brotherhood of man.

The basic difference between the two in their approach toward God is in connection with His oneness and unity. Jews do not recognize Jesus as the Messiah promised by the Scriptures, nor the inclusion of Jesus within the concept of the oneness and unity of God.

This fundamental difference, however, does not affect the influence of God upon the lives of Jew and Christian. Whether the Jews approach God directly, as they see it, or whether the Christians reach God through Jesus, as they believe, both seek to contact God and the ultimate goal of both is to reach God. Whichever the road, the end of the journey is God.

So that both religions, even in this respect, may reasonably be deemed to be similar in that adherents of each are seeking the same end—to reach God, the same God, the one God of all mankind, the one God of the universe.

Thus, it is apparent from the foregoing that the ethical aim of Jew and Christian is virtually the same. Each is seeking to bring about universal justice, righteousness and peace and the brotherhood of man.

Few worthwhile things come in life to him who merely waits. To attain our ends requires affirmative action. There has been stressed in the chapter on FREEDOM OF WILL that God has given us freedom of will so that we may do our own choosing, make our own choice. This gift, which we humans have received by grace of God, was given to us for a purpose. This purpose has been referred to and emphasized in various portions of the book.

If we believe that Jews and Christians have the same ethical goal in life, and if we desire to attain it, then we must exercise our freedom of will and strive to bring it about—by doing, by acting.

Christianity has been a great constructive force in speeding the time when we shall achieve this era on earth. By converting millions of pagans and teaching them to adopt its ethical principles, it has set many millions of human beings on the road leading to this goal.

We may fairly consider Jews and Christians as partners in this great enterprise for the greater glory of God and for the salvation of mankind on earth.

The common objective can be more effectively and more quickly accomplished through collaboration and coöperation of the partners. Any misunderstanding, disagreement and friction between them can be greatly reduced and perhaps completely eliminated, if both Jew and Christian were brought to fully understand that each group is seeking the same ethical result. Our rabbis, ministers and priests, our religious schools and places of public worship can aid materially if they but stress the similarities inherent in these two great religions in this respect and the deeper kinship that exists among all human beings, and omit emphasis on any apparent or technical differences.

Jews must coöperate and work closely to the fullest extent with their Christian brethren in every forward movement, economic, social, political and religious. Every such movement having for its aim the establishment of justice, righteousness and peace, must have the unrestricted and complete support of every Jew. This is so, regardless of the affiliation of those sponsoring or heading such movement and whether such movement be within or without any religious organization.

To illustrate, if the Catholic members of the community maintain certain organized charities, any drive for funds should receive full support and coöperation by Jews. If a Protestant branch of Christianity is constructing a home for their aged and infirm, this movement should have the complete support of the Jews.

The converse of the foregoing is likewise essential if we are to attain our mutual aim. Christians must coöperate and work with their Jewish brethren in every forward movement initiated by the Jews.

By concerted action, by mutual coöperation between

Jews and Christians, in good works, the ethical end sought by both will sooner be brought about.

It is largely upon the basis of the soul that we derive the concept of the brotherhood of man. By possessing a soul, each human being has a part of God within him. God is oneness and unity and we are all part of and embraced within such oneness and unity. Thus, each of us is related to God and so, through God, related to each other. The part of God in each human being is the link which makes all humanity brothers. As brothers, we must do unto others as we would have others do unto us, and we must love our neighbors as we love ourselves.

When Jews and Christians come to a full realization of this truth and, arm in arm, work together in bringing to this earth and to all its peoples, justice, righteousness and peace, we shall then attain the true brotherhood of man and we shall then have here on earth, the kingdom of God.

Chapter XXII

PRAYER

GOD does not need prayer. We humans need prayer. There is an urge within all of us to pray which goes beyond our reason.

It is not an uncommon experience among children of adolescent years, while in school, to mentally appeal to God asking for His help to pass examinations which they are about to take.

It is interesting to note that God is to children very much some entity which is readily accessible to them. Not only does the child instinctively appeal to God for help, he even makes a bargain with God. The child says to God, "if you will do thus and so for me, I promise to do thus and so." In discussions with children, we find that God has usually kept the bargain but the child has not. After the child has secured a passing mark, he forgets about God until the next examination comes around when he will again ask God for a favor.

This helps to illustrate the innate desire, the yearning and urge for prayer, of communing with God, of pleading with Him to help us. It has been previously pointed out that, in times of great stress, we instinctively turn to God. Danger, despondency, anguish, sorrow, discontent, a troubled heart, all bring out this impulse to pray. We appeal to Him, we petition Him, we supplicate Him for help. Here the adult as well does not attempt to reason whether he can approach God personally. He feels that reliance upon his own self is inadequate, that his knowledge and wisdom are insufficient, and he approaches God and appeals directly to Him, knowing, or perhaps only hoping, that God will deign to lend His ear and hear his prayer.

We humans feel so helpless at times, as in the case of parents with a son in war. We have only God to whom we can turn and to whom we can pray, beseeching Him to place His protecting arms around our boy and to return him safely to us. Prayer helps us to bear up under these great moments of stress. We ask God to incline His ear toward us and hear us.

When we petition God for help, our very act of prayer implies that we are appealing to a power beyond the natural laws. We cannot pray to a natural law asking it to operate in our favor. We, therefore, pray to something that is above and beyond the natural laws. Each person is endeavoring to build a definite pathway between himself and God.

This instinctive turning to God must have some solid and sound foundation and cannot be a mere whim or caprice of the human mind, and it is reasonable to conclude that there is this direct personal connection and relationship with God—between the individual and his God.

We cannot understand the benefits to be derived from prayer, without first experiencing them by praying. When man is inclined to stray from the doing of right, he can strengthen his determination to resist such straying. He can pray to God to create in him a clean heart and a right spirit. Prayer helps to banish evil thoughts and to purify, refine and ennoble our hearts. When God's intercession is asked for, He helps man to carry out his good intentions.

By praying, we keep constantly before us God's religious and ethical teachings, we keep them alive within us and this encourages and helps us to practice them.

By praying, we give outward expression to our inner feeling of reverence and love of God and of our thoughtfulness of Him and thankfulness to Him for all the favors He has bestowed upon us. Prayer is the voice of love, of pleading, of thanksgiving, of adoration, of friendship. When one's heart is opened to God, God can come in and He can then inspire and help. God cannot help us unless we give him the opportunity to do so. There must be coöperation with God if we want Him to help us. Prayer opens the door of our mind and heart to God.

Since, however, God is a God of justice, we cannot expect help from Him unless we have complied with His laws for the proper conduct of our lives. God is directly interested and concerned with each human being. With this comes the concomitant obligation of the individual, that he is responsible to God for his behavior and acts.

If we expect God to be our ally and our helper, we must perform our end of the bargain and comply with His laws and conduct our lives in the manner prescribed by God.

There is another phase of prayer which makes it worthwhile and necessary. The direct effect of prayer often is the change that takes place in man himself. Entirely aside from our communication with God through prayer, we strengthen and improve our personality with prayer. When we pray, there is an inflow of energy. Prayer ever brings us more strength, consolation and comfort, and, consciously or instinctively, helps us to organize ourselves to bring about the very accomplishment of our prayers.

Prayer in and of itself helps to give us fortitude in adversity, courage when danger threatens and confidence in ourselves when doubts spring up. It will quiet our fears, forebodings and misgivings, remove our false worries and morbid humors, and give us tranquility, serenity and patience.

They that confide in Him renew their strength.

Prayer is instinctively engaged in and is as natural as breathing. It is a natural function of man. It is one of the deepest impulses of man. We find it practiced in every form of society and in every religious belief. We should give it a trial and keep at it for a time. We shall then understand its influence on us.

When we try to curb the desire for prayer welling up within us, we hurt ourselves. We deprive ourselves of the opportunity offered to associate ourselves closely with God. When we feel the impulse for prayer, we should not inhibit it. On the contrary, we should place ourselves in a receptive mood and with all sincerity give ourselves up to carrying out this impulse of the soul. We should

yield readily and completely to this impulse and pray, and
then our hearts will be fired by it, and we shall come
closer to the Divinity.

To pray mechanically is equivalent to not praying.
This is true whether the prayer is in silent thought or
outwardly spoken. A mumbo-jumbo form of praying will
be of no avail.

For prayer to be effective, there must be utter sincerity
—we must know and comprehend what we say in our
prayers and we must be sincere in these statements—
otherwise, prayer has no value and we then neither communicate with God, nor uplift ourselves.

We may utter such prayers as instinctively rise from
within us. Our own imagination, our own command of
words, are often, however, insufficient and inadequate to
express to God the thoughts we wish to convey. The book
of Psalms supplies this need. The psalms embrace every
form of prayer that our heart urges us to utter. In some
portions of the Scriptures God speaks to man directly or
through the prophets, in some parts man speaks directly
to man, but in the psalms man attempts to communicate
directly with his God. In exalted language we human beings address ourselves to God.

Although the book of Psalms is partly an anthology of
the songs of a people, including war songs, holiday songs,
prayers written in battle, during illness and under the
stress of other circumstances, the psalms have, as their
motif, some form of declaration of our faith and belief in
the Almighty. All of them emphasize our dependence

upon and belief in our Maker. We acknowledge to God
the realization of our insignificance and the temporary
span of our life, as compared with His all-powerfulness
and eternity.

In the words of the prayer based upon the psalms,
which is part of the New-Year service: In truth thou art
their Creator, who knowest their nature, that they are
flesh and blood. As for man, he is from the dust and unto
dust will he return; he getteth his bread with the peril of
his life; he is like a fragile potsherd, as the grass that with-
ereth, as the flower that fadeth, as a fleeting shadow, as a
passing cloud, as the wind that bloweth, as the floating
dust, yea, as a dream that flieth away. But thou art the
King, the living and everlasting God— Thus we make
declaration to Him of our appreciation and gratitude.

It is not the manner of approach to God that counts,
but the spirit that accompanies it. Neither great passion
nor tearful pleading will help, unless there is accompanying sincerity and earnestness. We must approach God in
a spirit of humility. We must approach God with our
hearts wide open to receive Him. If we have committed
wrong, there must be sincere repentance and a real determination to conform to God's laws in the future.

We are sometimes deeply disappointed because we believe that our prayers have been unanswered. We cannot
understand why our requests, which seemed so reasonable
and right to us, have remained unheeded by God. We feel
that God has failed us. We do not realize that it is not

God who is found wanting, but it is ourselves who have asked for something we should not have. We often have this lack of understanding because we do not think through the possible reasons for non-compliance with our supplication.

Two persons may be asking at the same time for opposite things, and each one is certain that what he is asking for is right, and should be granted by God. One man is pleading for rain because his crop may be ruined on account of a drought. A man operating a nearby summer resort is praying for dry weather, as rain would seriously affect his business. One or the other must be disappointed. Assuming that God were acting in a finite way, he might deny the resort-keeper's prayer and grant the farmer's, because to do so would result in the greater good for the greater number.

In some instances, God may be conferring a greater favor upon us by denying our prayer. We may not realize it at the time but later we may even be grateful to Him for not having granted our prayer. A law school graduate may be deeply disappointed because his prayer to secure employment with a firm of attorneys has not been answered, as a result of which he is forced to practice his profession on his own account. Years later that law firm may have lost its law practice and ceased to function, while he, in the meantime, may have become successful.

The foregoing is, of course, a rather naïve way of explaining decision which appear to have been made by God. The truth of the matter is that it has not been given to man to fathom God's intentions and purposes.

We have the common illustration of two soldiers who are fighting on opposite sides. Each believes his cause to be just. Each prays for the success of his arms. God cannot grant the wishes of both. The defeated soldier may feel that he has been let down by God, that God has not made a just decision.

We cannot with our finite minds judge the justice of what God has done. His purposes and aims are not revealed to us. Knowing that there is purpose in the universe, we must have faith that God knows best. The ways of the Lord are inscrutable and it is not for us human beings to question His acts.

The more perfect an individual is, the closer and the more intimate is he with God and God with him. God is always as near to us as we want Him to be. If He appears to be far away, it is not God who is remote—it is we who are remote from Him.

We must purge our souls, our thoughts, our intentions, our words and our actions, from all evil. We must strive to be at one with God. When we reach that state, man is filled with joy and with a sense of security—prayer helps us to attain this end.

We must not think of praying as something to be done, only when we are in trouble and want God's help. We must not regard God as a genie who is subject to our beck and call, so that, when we rub the Aladdin's lamp, He will be at our elbow, ready to carry out our wishes. We must not develop the habit of praying to God only when we need Him, and of becoming unmindful of Him after our wishes are fulfilled. This is a narrow and utterly improper attitude to adopt and one that will surely bring disappointment, for we shall find that God does not act like the genie of Aladdin's lamp.

We must get to know God and let God get to know us. We must develop a true and sincere desire to commune with Him, not alone when we call upon Him for help, but at all other times. We should learn to pray when there is no external impulsion to do so. We should do it as a normal need to refresh our mind, our heart, our soul, just as normally as we eat and sleep to maintain our body.

We may regard our association with God as similar in some respects to our association with a friend. We do not consider our friendship as existing primarily for the purpose of securing favors or benefits. We derive from our friendships understanding, comradeship and a feeling of greater contentment with life. By prayer we can develop these same relations with God.

We also know that, in order to maintain a friendship, we must meet with our friends at intervals not too far apart—otherwise friendship may cool and finally end. This applies as well to our relationship with God.

We must learn to thank God for His many kindnesses and express our deep appreciation and gratitude for good health, happy home life, material success and the realization of our ambitions; we must make Him the confidant of our concerns, hopes and aspirations; we must make Him our confessor, to whom we confess our wrongful acts and pledge ourselves not to commit them again; we must develop a real joy in adoring Him; and we must consecrate ourselves to the duty of carrying out His will on earth.

These are the purposes of prayer and when we have learned to pray in this spirit, we shall then have reached the point of true association with God.

Chapter XXIII

PUBLIC WORSHIP

FROM almost the very inception of Judaism, there was the urge of the Jews to meet together in groups for the purpose of prayer. In the early days, they met at altars erected outdoors, where the sacrifices prescribed by the Torah were made. This practice ultimately led to the building by Solomon of the first temple in Jerusalem. After its destruction and during the Babylonian captivity in the sixth century before the present era, places of worship were constructed, where the Jews could meet to study and to pray together to their God. Thereafter wherever Jewish communities developed, places of public worship were constructed for these purposes.

The orthodox and conservative places of public worship are known as synagogues, while those of the reform division of the faith are called temples.

The meeting together in a place of public worship is not unique with the Jews. As far back as history goes, we read of congregations of peoples, assembled in their temples of worship.

Long before there was any scientific knowledge of psychology, those who acted as the leaders of religions knew from experience the psychological effect of group praying, and they wisely encouraged communal meetings. By praying to God, when alone, we cannot arouse within us that depth of religious feeling which comes when we pray in company with others. Emotion is readily transmitted by one to another, when people are together. Others, joining with us and undergoing the same emotions, stimulate our own emotions. Each person in the group in turn affects the other persons of the group. This is particularly so where the emotions are aroused through religious fervor.

It is thus apparent that when a person prays together with others, his feelings are much more likely to be deeply stirred than if he prays alone. He is more inclined to catch the spirit of the prayers. The absorption in and the contemplation of God of those around him, the sincerity of their praying, the attentiveness of the audience to the words of the leader of the congregation, the singing by the cantor or by a choir, all create in each individual a much greater and more fundamental effect because of its effect upon those around him.

In a place of public worship, the omnipresence of God is felt more than in any other place. The air appears to be surcharged with the spirit of the services and there is the feeling that God Himself is present in the house of worship. The temple actually becomes a house of God (Bethel) and God's spirit (Shekinah) pervades all within it.

Life teaches us to control our emotions, our instincts, our minds. We consider our personality developed to the extent to which we can control these three factors. One of the primary distinctions between ourselves and other forms of life is our ability of self-control.

To some extent, self-control means the exercise of inhibitions, that is, restraints upon ourselves. We are inhibited so much in life that, by the time we become mature, most of us are full of inhibitions which have become almost second nature with us, and great effort is required to throw them off. These inhibitions become so much a part of ourselves that, even when we pray, we find difficulty in letting ourselves go. It is the purpose of the house of public worship to enable us to overcome these inhibitions when praying, so that when we approach God in our prayers, we shall do so freely and completely with our entire heart and soul.

When we enter, we leave behind worldly ambitions and personal interests. We leave behind the distractions of home and business surroundings. All around us are persons praying as we are. Our minds become relaxed. Our grip on ego and personality is loosened. We withdraw from everyday life into the contemplation of our God. We forget our own small, individual lives. Our worries, our fears, the trials and tribulations of our everyday life, become less important; there is an ebb and flow of emotions; and we begin to share in common with others present, a spiritual life. Our self-respect, our dignity, are enhanced and deepened and our confidence in ourselves is strengthened.

Jews are a minority in all nations and in practically all the communities in which they reside. As the Sabbath brings about the periodical reunion of one's family, so the weekly service in the synagogue and temple helps to reunite all Israel. The common bond of the Jews is strengthened and their sense of loyalty to their people is deepened.

If Jews attend regularly the synagogue or temple, they meet and associate with and come to know many of their co-religionists. They realize that there are others who feel and believe as they do, and they develop a sense of solidarity with them. They develop the feeling that they belong. They create a fellowship of faith. There is a realization that they are a part of a greater life, that they are an integral part of a people who have survived in spite of all and who will survive to the end of time.

If they regularly worship publicly, they review and renew periodically the historical and religious life of their people. As they read and are told of the experiences of their forefathers through the ages, there is imbued within them a feeling of kinship and closeness with the past. The bond of union between the past and present is cemented. The past and the present become one continuous stream of life and appear to fuse, and the living become part of the eternal life of their people.

Attendance at a place of public worship develops unselfishness. The individual's prayers are not devoted solely to those concerning himself. He prays to God for the wellbeing of his brethren, for the welfare of all the people of his country and for all mankind. When he asks for forgiveness of sins, he asks for atonement not only for himself but also for all peoples.

The atmosphere of the house of God is helpful in bringing about a feeling of brotherliness. Praying together makes prayer so much more intimate and penetrating— it cleanses us from bitterness and anger toward others— it makes us more kindly disposed toward others—it develops a deeper sense of loyalty to and a greater love of our fellow man. We realize the interdependence of each human being with others and there is strengthened the relationship of man with man. Our personality must be affected for the better. This cleansing process must have its effect and we leave the place of worship a better person, in relationship to ourselves, to our family and to society.

There is one phase of public worship that is so deep in its significance and so profound as to seem almost supernatural in its effect. For the person who, in his youth, has regularly attended public worship with his parents, since passed on, attendance brings back vividly to his mind, and to his heart, his loving associations with them. He lives with them again, as if they were at his side. There crowd upon him memories as vivid and real almost as if there had been a resurrection of the souls of his parents and a joinder of their souls with his.

Most of us idealize our parents and, whether we know it or not, our thoughts of them make the fine things in life of greater value to us. The recollection of their goodness and kindness must ennoble our thoughts and must leave a permanent imprint within us.

There are certain designated occasions when Jews attend services in memory of their parents and of other loved ones who have passed on. For a period of eleven months, immediately following the loss of a parent, wife, husband, child, brother or sister, they are required to attend the morning, noon and evening services and recite the Kaddish prayer. On each anniversary date of their passing, attendance is also required and this prayer is recited. On the last day of each of the three principal festivals, Passover (Pesach), the Feast of the Weeks (Shabuoth) and the Feast of Tabernacles (Succoth) and also on the Day of Atonement (Yom Kippur), a part of the services, known as the Memorial Service, is especially set aside for prayer for the dead.

The Kaddish prayer is an important part of these special services. In the Kaddish prayer, no reference is made to the departed. It is rather a reaffirmation by the worshipper of his belief, faith and trust in God, and of his full and complete submission and obedience to God's will. During the Memorial Service, the worshipper recalls his beloved ones who have passed from the scene. He contemplates the purpose of life and the ultimate end of man, and his heart and soul are influenced for good.

We human beings are primarily social beings. We have an instinctive urge to mingle and associate with others. We are endowed by nature with the desire to live with others, and not alone. This urge is as true with respect to worship as it is in connection with other human relations. One can no more be a lone wolf in his religious observances than he can in his ordinary life. Attendance at a place of public worship satisfies this urge religiously, and we should endeavor to secure such satisfaction by experiencing the comradeship that exists among those who regularly attend.

There is another vital reason for attending a place of public worship. Few persons organize for themselves an orderly manner of approach toward God. Individual prayer is ordinarily spontaneous, arising out of some bereavement, grave danger or serious crisis. It is usually in the form of supplication, pleading for God's help.

The synagogue and temple have developed a ritual which is intended to arouse the varied spiritual feelings of the worshipper, not confined solely to an emotional appeal to God for help. These spiritual feelings include— thanksgiving, the worshipper thanking God for His favors and for His goodness—confession, the worshipper confessing his wrongful acts and praying for forgiveness and earnestly resolving not to sin again—adoration, the worshipper expressing to God his love for Him—and consecration, the worshipper consecrating himself to God and pledging himself to live a Godly life. The service is arranged to cover each of the above forms. The prayers follow in orderly sequence, and the emotions that may be aroused by prayer are, in this manner, fully covered.

No medium of human expression can so exalt a person

as that of song. Song is an important part of the synagogue and temple service. Chanting and singing by the cantor, sometimes alone, sometimes in unison with the congregation, help to elevate the soul and to cause the worshipper to forget the routine of his daily existence and to deeply feel and live the religious emotions. Music is a language of its own, and the music of the synagogue, the ancient chants and hymns, stir those present to their very souls. Selections from the book of Psalms are made use of throughout the prayer book. In the inspired and sublime lines of the psalms, the congregation speaks directly to God.

Some of the prayers are read aloud in responsive form. The rabbi or cantor alternates with the congregation in reciting the lines. Each worshipper's attention is concentrated on the text so that he may follow the reading correctly, and he participates in speaking the words, in unison with the entire congregation. He thus becomes completely absorbed in and uplifted by the service.

The sermon, an ancient institution, arouses the minds of those present and makes them think of things religious. An eloquent rabbi can move his listeners to their depths and can make religion a living and vital force for them. In addition to reminding his congregation of the teachings of their religion, which, when read, may sometimes appear abstract in form, the rabbi can have them assume flesh and blood and life, when explained by illustration. The rabbi can also vitalize the teachings by interpreting them in the light of present conditions and, in turn, he can bring new meaning and understanding to the events of the day by applying to them the precepts of God.

The Sabbath services include a reading from the Torah. A portion of it is read each week. The reading is so divided that the Torah is completely covered over a period of three years or over one year, the latter now being the usual procedure. There is also read a selection from the Prophets, one of the main subdivisions of the Scriptures, such selection usually having some reference to the subject matter of the portion of the Torah read that day. Accordingly, by regularly attending the synagogue or temple on the Sabbath, the worshipper will re-read the entire Torah each year and thus keep God's laws ever fresh in his mind.

In the conservative and reform divisions of the faith, the services usually end with the priestly benediction recited by the rabbi: The Lord bless thee and keep thee; the Lord make His face to shine upon thee, and be gracious unto thee; the Lord lift up His countenance upon thee, and give thee peace. In the orthodox branch, the priestly benediction is recited during the service. The entire personality of the worshipper is deeply affected and moved and he feels an inner glow which stays with him long after he has left the synagogue or temple.

It is not essential for an individual to regularly attend a place of public worship, in order to comply with and live up to the principles of his religion. If, however, religion is to be an important part of each Jew's personality, and God is to be for him a living God, if he is to refresh himself religiously and give to himself the active desire and urge to live a Godly life, then he should regularly attend a synagogue or temple.

Each person cannot individually develop, within the same period of time, the deep religious fervor described in this chapter. Attendance at public worship may bring it about quickly in some, while with others it may be a longer process. One cannot expect to derive the uplift and the other benefits by a single visit or by irregular visits. The feeling of comradeship with and closeness to God and absorption in Him will develop only with regular attendance. If one expects to secure benefits from public worship, he must systematically prepare himself to receive them.

Whether the period be short or long, we must qualify ourselves by regular attendance and we must cultivate the habit of such periodical attendance and participation. Then, just as the day surely follows the night, we shall each of us derive from our public worship the benefits upon which we have dwelt. We may compare the development of our emotions religiously to those developed musically. Some of us, hearing opera for the first time, derive little enjoyment from the performance; but after regular attendance over a period of time, we develop a genuine and deep emotional appreciation for this form of musical expression. So it is with prayer.

Sometimes a person attending a synagogue or temple leaves the service disappointed. The service has left him indifferent and perhaps even cold. This may have been caused by the manner in which it was conducted at the place of worship which he attended. The synagogue and temple, after all, are human institutions, and the manner and effect of the service vary with each place of worship. Each Jew should attempt to find a synagogue or temple where he will derive the emotional uplift it should give to him.

Moreover, when disappointment is experienced in a service, the fault may not be that of the place of worship, but that of the worshipper. He may not have attended regularly; he may not yet have developed a receptive mood; he may not yet have opened up his inner self to receive the benefits of the service. Each person must qualify himself by regular attendance. If he does, he will then assuredly experience that emotional consolation, that satisfaction of the heart and that spiritual uplift which come to all who regularly attend a place of public worship.

It makes no difference whether one attends an orthodox, conservative or reform place of worship. Each is a sanctuary for prayer. They are all houses of God devoted to God's service, intended to bring to each person the spiritual elevation which comes from synagogue and temple service. The differences among these branches of Judaism are more apparent than real. Only the manner of approach, the ritual and procedure of the service, may vary. The beliefs and principles are fundamentally the same.

God loves all His children and will hear them and will care for them, be they orthodox, conservative or reform.

Chapter XXIV

THE SABBATH

THE opportunity to pray regularly and periodically, the necessity for which has been so greatly stressed in the previous chapter, is afforded by the Sabbath.

The Torah appears to set aside the Sabbath largely as a day of rest so that those who toil shall have at least one day each week to rebuild themselves physically. Six days may the individual labor and do his work, but the seventh day is the Sabbath, in honor of God, the Eternal, and on that day the individual must do no work, neither he, nor his sons, his daughters, nor his cattle nor the stranger who may be part of his household.

The implications of the Sabbath are, however, much more significant. It is recited in the book of Exodus that when God spoke to Moses, He instructed him to inform the Israelites that they must keep the Sabbath as a token that God had hallowed them, and that the keeping of the Sabbath by the Israelites was a binding pact between Him and them for all time.

Thus the Sabbath day is a day of sanctification. It is a day of deep religious significance to the Jews—it is a day specially fixed by God, on which they are reminded of and recall their bond and relationship with God, and on which they turn their thoughts and hearts to Him and to His laws.

The rabbis and scholars realized the deeper significance of this day. They realized that mind and memory are often dimmed by time, that the laws of God may lose some of their vitality if they are not periodically recalled. They accordingly stressed the importance of the observance of the Sabbath to such an extent that, with the exception of the Day of Atonement, the Sabbath days came to be considered the holiest of the year and the most important to observe.

The Torah also speaks of the Sabbath as symbolic of the creation of the world. The Sabbath also commemorates the departure of the Jews from Egypt, because during their bondage they were not given any weekly day of rest. They are thus reminded that God is the Creator of the universe and the Redeemer of the Israelites. And so they give thanks to God on the Sabbath because He has created them and redeemed them.

The Sabbath is the day dedicated to God. During the first six days of the week Jews provide for their material requirements but, on the seventh day, they care for their spiritual needs. When Jews attend the synagogue on Saturday, they take time off to think religiously, to meditate, to feel God, to get close to Him. Attendance at the synagogue or temple on the Sabbath can be considered as a date with God. Jews keep their date with Him weekly and thus renew their close association with Him.

When the Jews lived together as a nation and later when they were dispersed over the whole globe, but continued living together in smaller groups, generally in ghettos, the public opinion of their fellow Jews made Sabbath attendance by all, mandatory.

Notwithstanding the serious disadvantages and disabilities suffered by the Jews when segregated and living in ghettos, they were in a sense compensated for these restrictive conditions. Religion was not to them a vague, indefinite, abstract part of their lives, but a living, vital and dominant force. Having little to distract them, it was their solace and their comfort. It was as much a part of themselves and of their lives as their very being.

With the removal of the Jew from the ghetto, with his social, economic and political emancipation and with the coming of comparatively complete freedom from restriction, attendance at the synagogue became voluntary. With the Jew participating in the general life of the whole community, with its manifold activities attracting and intriguing him, his religion became of less importance to him, and his interest and ardor for it waned. There were many distractions that took his mind away from Sabbath observance.

This is especially true today when, because of the rapid tempo of work and life, many Jews are prone to lose sight of the importance to them of religion and give up regular Sabbath attendance. In the struggle for existence in the hurly-burly of life, they are so absorbed in their daily work that God's laws become blurred and hazy and are often even forgotten.

Moreover, in the present state of society, living in a land where they are but a small minority, and where they are constantly in close and intimate association, in their working and social life, with non-Jews, Jews find it difficult and often impossible to adhere strictly to the requirements of the Sabbath.

They should, nevertheless, attempt to observe the day as far as they can and they should make a special endeavor to attend synagogue service on the morning of the Sabbath. If this is done, they will renew and keep alive that close relationship with God, and so sanctify their lives as to derive the rich benefits which Judaism can give to each and all of them.

The Sabbath begins Friday at sunset, as the day runs from sunset to sunset in the Jewish calendar. The Sabbath is ushered in by the lighting of candles and a prayer by the mistress of the house. The evening meal starts with a prayer (Kiddush), recited by the master of the house, praising God for sanctifying the Sabbath, and with the drinking of the wine and the cutting of the bread (Challah). It is customary to have the entire family present.

The ceremony, though simple, is beautiful and impressive, and for those who have regularly participated in this weekly festive meal and family reunion, it is something which is unforgettable. There is a spirit of devoutness, of reverence, of solidarity and unity among the members of the family and an intangible sense of the closeness of God, which is felt, but which cannot be described.

Those who cannot or do not observe the Sabbath day by attending synagogue or temple and refraining from work, are especially urged to observe this Friday evening ceremonial and meal.

Sabbath today furnishes the opportunity of suspending the normal busy working life and returning again to the contemplation of God and His laws.

It would almost seem that each individual is in need of regular weekly exercise, religiously, to maintain a deeply conscious religious feeling and fervor. The weekly reaffirmation of his religious principles and beliefs and of his ethical ideals helps to keep them consciously before him at all times.

The prohibition against almost any form of labor on the Sabbath has, for its underlying purpose, the intention of freeing the individual from all labor, thereby enabling him to contemplate his religion. He is given again and again, on each Sabbath day, the opportunity of reminding himself of the ever-presence of God, and of renewing a conscious relationship with Him. He cleanses his soul. He refreshes his soul. He is uplifted. He detaches his thoughts from worldly things and places his hope in things to come. He becomes engrossed in God. He communes again with God and renews his vows with God and he becomes fully aware again of those great principles which must govern his life and the lives of all peoples, if he and all humanity are to secure the maximum of happiness.

We must not, however, receive the impression that the Sabbath is a day of austerity, of gloom or sadness. On the contrary, Judaism teaches that, notwithstanding its solemnity and holiness, the Sabbath is a day of joy and happiness. The service at the synagogue and temple is one of earnestness and sincerity and of a losing of oneself in the contemplation of God. But the prayers stress the happiness of life, the songs are songs of thankfulness and gratitude to God for His many favors, and the atmosphere of the synagogue and temple on the Sabbath day is one of optimism and gladness.

Only a part of the day is spent in prayer. Being freed from his daily pursuits, the individual can mingle and associate with his children, with the other members of his family and with his friends. During the week, he is away at work, his children are at school and the other members of the family are busy with their daily routine. Friends and neighbors are also freed on the Sabbath from their daily occupations. The Sabbath is a day of reunion and of renewal of all close and intimate relationships and associations.

His close communion with God, the outpouring of his love and affection upon his family, the receipt by him of their love and affection, the binding more closely of the bonds of friendship and neighborliness, with his friends and neighbors—all in all, it is a day that enables the Jew to give himself up wholly to worthwhile things and to drinking deeply at the fountain of life.

Chapter XXV

LIFE—A THRILLING ADVENTURE

As we look about us, it appears that man is the most important creation of God. All other forms of life are created to enable man to secure his sustenance, to assist him in his labor and to help him derive joy from living.

Man is given the power to subdue and control all the other forms of life. Although his strength is infinitely less than that which the forces of nature can exert, or with which plant and animal life are endowed, nevertheless, man is given the mental faculty to bend all of these to his will for his comfort, benefit and happiness. Man overcomes the frailty of his body, he overcomes his petty strength and he becomes the giant of the world.

This conclusion is not the result of man's conceit or the exaggeration of his importance. It is based upon the actual experience of our domination and control of nature through the power of our mind.

God's intention is to make his supreme creation, man, happy. He has given to man a code of laws which, if universally obeyed, will bring about this happy state.

In order, however, to derive real happiness, the human being must strive for it. The ultimate aim of God appears to be that man shall attain the maximum happiness through his own efforts and merit. We have only to look to our own experiences to find that we derive the greatest joy from those accomplishments for which we have to strive. Things that come to us, without effort on our part, are not appreciated as much as those which we acquire as a result of striving for them. This is one of the explanations for the creation of man as a free agent.

God has furnished man with the laws that should regulate his life. He thus places man in a position where he must act affirmatively in abiding by those laws in order to attain happiness. The laws are so broad that compliance requires active effort on our part and often self-control, inhibitions and sacrifice. In making this effort and in exercising this restraint and in complying, we derive great satisfaction which, in turn, leads to happiness.

Our adventure starts with a miracle, our birth. Out of inanimate and inorganic matter, there is born the sense of entity and personality, and we become the possessor of a soul. From the very first moment of life, we enter upon an adventure, not knowing what each future day, hour or even minute will bring. The experience of the past and our environment, which have left their impress upon us, the improvement of our mind through education, our religious teachings, the strengthening of our body, all are the armor with which we gird ourselves to meet the battle of life. As we attain maturity, we leave the protecting wings of our parents, and we go out into the world, relying upon our own selves. We are prepared for the hazards, joys and sorrows that lie ahead and which we must face.

We must have faith in our ability to carry on and we must have the courage, determination and daring to see it through, no matter what the obstacles may be, regardless of what life may have in store for us. We must look forward to each task with pleasurable anticipation, instead of with misgiving and worry in our heart; and after the task is completed, we must have the confidence and assurance in ourselves that the task has been well done.

We must have faith in our family, in our friends, in our ideals and in ourselves. Faith is indispensable to life, as our entire life is built on faith, and without it, we cannot truly live. In the same manner, we must have faith in God. We shall then have the patience and the endurance to overcome all the obstacles that life may place in our path, and we can then take them all in our stride, with God walking at our side.

During youth, we are inclined to develop our own views of life and our own thoughts on religion. Doubt by youth is not an uncommon phenomenon. During childhood, we accept the religion of our parents and their views are inculcated in us. It is as natural for the child to do so as it is for him to look to his parents for food, shelter and protection.

When we attain adolescence, we mature physically and mentally, and also spiritually. We develop the ambition of earning our own livelihood and of having our own views and opinions in connection with our daily lives. In the same manner, we become unwilling to take on faith the religious views of our parents. We want to think them out for ourselves. Our dissatisfaction with taking our religion on faith may lead to doubt and skepticism.

Youth is often defiant of tradition. Sometimes this attitude may be caused by a deep-seated prejudice which we may not have been aware of at the time of its creation. It may have been caused perhaps by the manner in which we have been taught the ritual of our religion, or by the form or manner of worship conducted at the places of public worship we attended. We may have considered the service tedious, our attendance may have been compulsory and regarded as onerous. Some may not have had any religious training or may have had only an indifferent one. Religious atmosphere may have been lacking in the home. Whatever the reason, we sometimes develop in our youth an almost antagonistic feeling and frame of mind toward religion generally.

Many in later years do not take the trouble or make the effort to think it through. Unless we do so, we deprive ourselves of the great opportunity of formulating a correct view of the true meaning of life and of the way of life taught by our religion, and we thereby lose the opportunity of securing for ourselves the contentment and inner peace that might have been ours for all the mature years of our life. It is one of the duties to ourselves, when we attain maturity, to take the time and to make a strong conscious effort to find again for ourselves the religion of our fathers and to make it part of our own very lives.

After we reach maturity, fear is often the poisoner of happiness and colors our activities. During working hours our minds are occupied with our daily labors and other tasks, part of the routine of our lives. During our leisure time we are taken up with our family, our friends, our other interests, and with various forms of relaxation and diversion. If the thought of death obtrudes itself upon our minds, we readily dismiss it. But in the stillness of the night, the thought of death often returns.

To live and not to feel the thrill of living is like not living at all. We must not be afraid to live as we must not be afraid to die. Fear benumbs and paralyzes us and restricts and limits the development of our personality, but faith gives us encouragement, vitalizes us and brings out all of our potentialities. If we have fear, no matter what advantages nature or society have given to us, we shall still remain unhappy, while faith will help us to derive a maximum of pleasure and enjoyment from these advantages.

If we are to be happy, we must find life good, we must have a zest for life and be in love with life. We can only attain this point when we have removed fear through true and sincere belief.

We all have periods of doubt, of keen disappointment, and we even experience occasions when we feel completely crushed. We must then exercise self-control and courage to sustain us and enable us to bridge and live through these periods and we must never lose our faith.

Faith in ourselves, faith in our God, faith in the purposefulness of life, faith built on the hope in a future that will come beyond life—will enable us to live a life of contentment and peace, and will make our occupations and undertakings not fearful tasks but—a thrilling adventure.

If life is to be good, we must follow the precept of the prophet Micah: It hath been told thee, O man, what is good, and what the Lord doth require of thee— Only to do justly, and to love mercy, and to walk humbly with thy God.

And when life's adventure reaches its end—we can then look forward with hope and even with anticipation to a new and more thrilling adventure to come.